How Effective Executives Interview

How Effective Executives Interview

Walter R. Mahler

 1976

DOW JONES-IRWIN   Homewood, Illinois   60430

First Printing, January 1976

ISBN 0-87094-113-5
Library of Congress Catalog Card No. 75-27606
Printed in the United States of America

To Martha and Michael

Preface

INTERVIEWING is a skill. So is golfing. Can one learn golfing skill by reading a book? It is unlikely! Can one learn interviewing skill by reading a book? It is unlikely! Why then should a book on executive interviewing be written? Primarily because:

1. Executives can decline to play golf if they wish, but they have to interview whether they are ready to do so or not.
2. Most executives have had considerable experience on the giving and receiving end of interviews.
3. Those executives with a modest level of ability may find the principles in this book to be of help in raising their ability level.
4. The book can be used as a text for an educational course. Cases for role playing are included.

Interviewing is a process which must be carried out with considerable frequency by every executive. Yet few executives have ever had any skill-training in interviewing. Few executives have well worked out processes to use.

In this book attention will be given to five types of interviews:

Selection interviews.

Performance interviews.

Counseling interviews.

Career discussions.

Removal interviews.

Effective interviewing requires that one master the mechanics of these interviews. Appropriate processes will be suggested for each type of interview. These processes have been tested and perfected by scores of executives over a period of years. But more than mechanics is needed. The dynamic aspect of interviewing requires knowledge and application of principles, guidelines, and theories. Here again, practical guidelines are provided for each type of interview.

In addition, we have distilled from the behavioral research literature those findings we consider most relevant to executive interviewing. Finally, our use of executive surveys over more than a decade enables us, in many instances, to provide data of the present state of the art of interviewing.

This book is written for the executive who is concerned about his or her competence as an interviewer. The principles and guidelines aren't easy ones. It will take diligent effort to convert the written word into a verbal skill. We foresee executives reading the book to prepare for an interview. They can also read it after an interview to facilitate self-criticism.

The book is also written for those members of the management development and training fraternity who want to provide effective skill training. All the material needed to design a solid interviewing course, or courses, has been included. If we have any trade secrets they are in the book!

This book is intended to complement an earlier one which the late Bill Wrightnour and I prepared several years ago, entitled *Executive Continuity*. We stressed the need for more and better coaching by managers, but in that book we were not able to offer helpful suggestions that this book provides.

I am especially grateful to the many executives who, over a period of years, have participated in programs and courses with me. Their subsequent experimentation gave the processes and principles presented here a good workout. Considerable modification took place. It is impossible to personally recognize the score of executives who have helped pave the way for this book. I am deeply indebted to all of them.

A special contribution has been made by the participants in my Advanced Management Skills Program for General Managers. One week of the eight-week program is devoted to executive interviewing. Each participant is expected to apply the skills developed by the use of role-playing within his or her organization. Their efforts, in perfecting their interviewing have provided valuable clues for our preparation of this book.

December 1975   WALTER R. MAHLER

Contents

You Want to Talk about. Stress Why It Is in the Interest of the Subordinate to Change. Explain a Change Will Be Necessary. Test for Acceptance by Asking for a Plan of Action. Provide for Follow-Up.

Almost All Individuals Have a Strong Concern about Their Future. Managers Want to Talk about Their Future with Their Superior; Same Managers Are Reluctant to Talk with Their Subordinates about Their Future. It Is Not Necessary or Desirable to Tell Individuals They Will or Will Not Be Promoted. A Primary Outcome of a Career Discussion Should Be an Increase in Realism. Career Discussions Should Assist Individuals to Look at Themselves in Terms of the Requirements of Higher Positions. Career Discussions Are More Productive if They Precede Critical Decisions. A Career Discussion Is Important in Developing Future Talent, in Motivating Talent Which Is Not Going Any Higher, and in Avoiding or Overcoming Obsolescence. Career Discussions Are a Tangible Indication of Concern for a Subordinate. Executives Who Have a Reputation for Furthering the Careers of Their Subordinates, Have an Advantage in Attracting and Keeping Top Talent.

Exploratory Discussion in Terms of One's Current Position. Exploratory Discussion in Terms of Future Positions. Career Discussion in Terms of a Specification for a General Position. Career Discussion in Terms of a Specification for a Given Position.

The Misconduct Decision. The "Elimination of the Position" Removal. The "Nonperformance" Decision.

part one

Pertinent Behavioral Research

INTERVIEWING is a means to an end. That end has something to do with the behavior of an individual. The individual will usually be a subordinate. When you are conducting a selection interview you are anticipating or predicting future behavior. In a performance interview you are concentrating on behavior which is related to currently expected results. In a counseling interview you are hoping to get a change in undesired behavior. In a career discussion you are dealing with the interesting interrelationship of aspiration and ability of an individual. Finally, a removal interview requires an individual change from his or her current position. As one scans this list of outcomes, the importance of having a good understanding of the human behavior which is involved certainly becomes apparent if you expect to be successful in getting the change in behavior you desire.

We will be suggesting numerous processes for interviews. We will provide guidelines and tactics to use in the inter-

1

views. This adds up to the mechanics of interviewing. Mechanics are important, but more than mechanics are needed if the desired behavioral outcomes are to be attained. This brings us to the dynamics of interviewing. The dynamics of interviewing require understanding and insight into the behavior of individuals. It also involves understanding the behavior on both sides of the superior/subordinate relationship.

Entire books have been written on the subject of human behavior. In fact, entire books have been written on one facet of human behavior. It will be necessary to be selective about the behavioral research findings to be considered. I will limit myself to those findings which I feel are most helpful in the types of interviewing under consideration.

In Chapter 1 attention will be given to the dynamics of the superior/subordinate relationship. You have often asked yourself, Why does a given subordinate act in a certain manner? What are the subordinate's motivations? Is it possible to get a change in behavior? What influence can I have on the behavior of a subordinate?

The dynamics of the superior/subordinate relationship rests on the basic dependence of the subordinate on the superior. One way this might be diagrammed is:

The diagram implies a "big," dominant superior and a "small," dependent subordinate. The diagram might also be set up as follows:

The implication of a hierarchy is necessarily implied. How-ever, the subordinate is seen as "independent," of compa-rable "size," and interacting with the superior. Chapter 1 de-votes considerable attention to the things a superior must provide to get this shift from dependency to independence. We will argue that such a shift is necessary if the perform-ance of a subordinate is to be optimized.

Chapter 2 looks at the importance of a position to an in-dividual. Interviews have to do with an individual and a position. The selection interview can be viewed from two views:

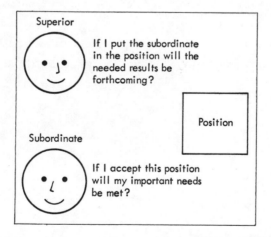

We will look at the meaning of work to an individual. A posi-tion will be seen as of great significance to the incumbent. Many of one's most critical needs are fulfilled by the position one occupies. We also will look at the critical role of one's self-concept in relation to a position.

In Chapter 3 attention will be directed to the behavioral aspects of satisfactory performance. As noted in the diagram above, this is a primary concern of the superior.

1

Superior/Subordinate Relationship

THE FUNDAMENTAL CHARACTERISTICS of the superior/subordinate relationship are identical whether one talks of a first-level superior and his or her manager, or a vice president and the president. There are, to be sure, differences in the content of the relationship, and in the relative importance of personal characteristics, at different levels of an organization. The underlying aspects, however, are common to all levels of management.

THE DEPENDENCE OF THE SUBORDINATE

The outstanding characteristic of the relationship between a superior and a subordinate is the latter's dependence upon the superior for the satisfaction of his or her needs. In a fundamental and pervasive sense, a subordinate is dependent upon a superior for one's job; for the continuity of one's employment; for promotion with its accompanying satisfactions in the form of increased pay, responsibility, and prestige; and for a host of other personal and social satisfactions to be obtained in one's position.

This dependence is not adequately recognized by many

5

executives. For one thing, it is not consistent with some of our basic social values. Emphasis is usually placed upon the importance of the subordinate's own efforts in achieving the satisfaction of needs. Nevertheless, the dependence is real, and subordinates are not unaware of it. Surveys of attitudes invariably place "fair treatment by superiors" toward the top of the list of factors influencing job satisfaction.

Psychologically, the dependence of a subordinate upon a superior is a fact of extraordinary significance, in part because of its emotional similarity to the dependence characteristic of another earlier relationship—that between the child and one's parents. The great popularity of Transaction Analysis, with its stress upon the roles of child, adult, and parent, attests to the pervasiveness of dependency as a concern of people in general.

The adult subordinate's dependence upon superiors actually reawakens certain emotions and attitudes which were part of one's childhood relationship with one's parents, and which apparently have long since been outgrown. The adult is usually unaware of the similarity because most of this complex of childhood emotions has been repressed. Although the emotions influence one's behavior, they are not accessible to consciousness under ordinary circumstances.

Adults often consider it absurd to compare these two relationships, but one cannot observe human behavior in business (a hierarchal organization) without being struck by the fundamental similarity between the two situations. You can likely recall an executive saying: "Those two executives who are fighting with each other are certainly acting childishly." Another executive may say: "I wonder why a given subordinate agrees with me even when I am wrong." Some executives are surprised when they assume a higher position to find they are cut off from free-flowing communications.

There are certain inevitable consequences of the depend-

ence of the subordinate upon a superior. The success or failure of the relationship depends on the way in which these consequences are handled. The job performance of subordinates
is greatly influenced by the dependence of a subordinate upon
a superior. An understanding of these consequences provides
a more useful basis than the usual "rules of thumb" for being
considerate of a subordinate. The consequences of the dependence of the subordinate will be discussed under two main
headings: (1) the necessity for security in the work situation,
and (2) the necessity for self-realization or independence.

THE NECESSITY FOR SECURITY
IN THE WORK SITUATION

Subordinates will struggle to protect themselves against
real or imagined threats to the satisfaction of their needs in
the work situation. Analysis of this protective behavior suggests that the actions of superiors are frequently perceived as
the source of threats. Before subordinates can believe that it
is possible to satisfy their needs in the work situation, they
must acquire a convincing sense of security in their dependent
relationship with their superiors.

Management has recognized the financial aspects of this
need for security and has attempted to provide for it by
means of many, so-called, fringe benefit plans, such as employees retirement plans and health and accident insurance.
However, the meeting of financial needs doesn't really come
to grips with the need for emotional security which results
from being dependent upon the judgments, the decisions, and,
often, the whims of one's superior.

McGregor[1] is well known for his Theory X and Theory Y.*

------

* A bibliography in Part Seven provides information on each of the
references. These references are listed in the sequence in which they are
mentioned in the book.

I consider his insight into the dynamics of the superior/subordinate relationship to be equally provocative. McGregor[2] suggests that there are three conditions needed for a sense of security:

1.   An atmosphere of approval.
2.   Numerous types of knowledge.
3.   Consistent discipline.

When one considers what is needed for the emotional security to be really achieved in a hierarchial organization, it seems to me that there are two other requirements which should be added to McGregor's list: (4) the position one occupies must be needed, and (5) one's organization must be successful or have a good possibility of becoming successful.

Let's consider each of these conditions in turn, because they have great significance for the five basic types of executive interviews featured in this book.

An Atmosphere of Approval

The first and most important of the five conditions needed for a sense of security is an "atmosphere of approval" which is created by the superior. This atmosphere is rerevealed not by what the superior does but by the manner in which things are done and by the underlying attitude implied toward subordinates. It is relatively independent of the strictness of the superior's discipline, or the standards of performance which the superior demands.

A divisional vice president was in the habit of speaking gruffly and intemperately to subordinates. However, the executive had selected each one of them. They had worked together for years. Each individual felt he or she was needed and respected. So, in this context, the executive's habits didn't have any adverse impact. Subsequently, the divisional vice president was appointed chief executive. As chief executive, all of the new subordinates were "inherited." Within a short period of time the chief executive was amazed to get reports that executives were afraid of their new "chief," that one was suffering nervous strain, and several were thinking of leaving. The subordinates did not have an atmosphere of approval as a working foundation for interpreting the gruff, abrupt mannerisms of their new superior.

Security for subordinates is possible only when they know they have the genuine approval of their superior. If the atmosphere is equivocal, or one of disapproval, they can have no assurance that their needs will be satisfied, regardless of what they do. In the absence of a genuine attitude of approval, subordinates feel threatened, fearful, insecure. Even neutral and innocuous actions of the superior are regarded with suspicion. Effective discipline is impossible, high standards of performance cannot be maintained, "sabotage" of the superior's efforts is quite possible. Resistance, antagonism, and, occasionally, open rebellion are the consequences.

Numerous Types of Knowledge

In his initial treatise McGregor[3] presented an a priori list of the kind of knowledge he deemed of consequence to subordinates. His list included the following:

1. Knowledge of overall company policy and management philosophy.
2. Knowledge of procedures, rules, and regulations.

3. Knowledge of the requirements of the subordinate's own job; the subordinates duties, responsibilities, and place in the organization.
4. Knowledge of the personal peculiarities of the subordinate's immediate superior.
5. Knowledge by the subordinate of the superior's opinion of his or her performance.
6. Advance knowledge of changes that will affect the subordinate.

Over the last five years, we have asked several thousand salaried personnel, both managerial and nonmanagerial, to indicate how important various job conditions were to them. Results pertaining to knowledge items are presented below.

Knowledge Item	Percent Saying Item Is Either "Very Important" or "Important"
Knowing your organization's goals and objectives	100
Having a good idea of what is expected of you on your job	96
Knowing what your manager thinks of your performance	91
Receiving information about what is going on in the organization	90

I should like to merge the two lists at this point to provide one list of the types of knowledge which is most important to a subordinate's sense of security. The list follows:

1. Knowing one's organizational goals.
2. Having a good idea of just what is expected of one in one's position.

3. Knowing what one's manager thinks of one's performance.
4. Receiving information about what is going on in one's organization.
5. Advance knowledge of changes that may affect the subordinate.
6. Knowledge of organizational "environmental" factors.
7. Knowledge of the personal "peculiarities" of the immediate superior.

Let's consider each type of knowledge briefly.

Knowing One's Organizational Goals. The term goal is defined in many different ways. For our purposes we propose to define goals as the results, the outcomes an organization expects to reach. The outcomes may be short term or long term. They may be stated precisely or in general terms. Examples of goals might include the following:

1. We will double sales in five years.
2. One half of our sales will be in defense and half in non-defense businesses.
3. We will operate on a global basis.
4. We will establish our own distribution system.
5. Our quality will be the best in the industry.
6. All employees will have an equal opportunity for development and advancement.

Why are goals so important to an individual? There are many reasons. Goals—:

1. Define the direction the organization is going.
2. Imply the organization knows where it is going.
3. Demonstrate that leadership exists.
4. Enable a subordinate to adapt his or her efforts to contribute directly to the overall goals.

5. Provide an individual with a basis for discerning whether his or her needs will be met.
6. Tell whether an organization is growing or contracting with its implications for the future.
7. Helps one to decide if one's initial choice of an organization was a wise one.

How well do executives do when it comes to providing knowledge of goals? We have data from more than 25 business and industrial organizations which suggests the answer is not very reassuring. We have made use of a Coaching Practices Survey for more than a decade. More than 5,000 managers from top level through to first level have completed the survey. The survey measures the frequency with which 45 different coaching, or supervisory, practices are accomplished as seen by subordinates.

Consider the following:

Has your superior informed you of his own objectives?	Only 45 percent say their superior "almost always" or "frequently" does this.

This result suggests that the prescription that knowledge of goals is needed is an easy one for McGregor or myself to make. Getting this to happen is a challenge.

Having a Good Idea of Just What Is Expected of One in One's Position. What is expected of an individual in a position can be defined in several ways. One can be expected to assume a responsibility for carrying out specific tasks or assignments. One can be expected to achieve certain end results. One can be expected to exercise certain authority. Expectations can also be defined in terms of a role one is to fulfill. Often these expectations are systematized in the form of documents. Tasks are included in a job description. Results are included in a goals document. One's authority is defined in an authority document. One's role is outlined in a charter or scope document.

Why is knowing what is expected of one so important a type of knowledge? Individuals recognize they remain employed as long as (1) there is work which needs to be done, and (2) they are doing the work satisfactorily. In addition, most individuals have a pride in accomplishment. They prefer to be able to judge when they have a right to feel proud of their accomplishments.

How well do executives do in providing subordinates with knowledge of what is expected of them? The results, in our Coaching Practices Survey, are quite positive.

Consider the following data:

1. How well do you understand what is expected of you in your current position?	Seventy-five percent say they have a "good" or "very good" understanding.
2. Do you and your superior agree on the most important goals you are expected to accomplish?	Seventy-four percent say they are in "full agreement" or in "full agreement with few exceptions."

It is encouraging to see that this vital knowledge requirement is being fulfilled so well. The higher one gets in an organization, the more you would be concerned about the one fourth who aren't so confident of what is expected of them.

Knowing What One's Manager Thinks of One's Performance. This knowledge has several facets. The facets are reflected in the questions subordinates ask themselves:

1. Does my manager think I am doing a good job?
2. Is my manager dissatisfied with any aspect of my performance?
3. Does my manager expect me to do more?
4. Am I likely to be criticized by my manager?
5. Am I doing the job in the way my manager expects?
6. Haven't I earned a word of praise or some recognition?
7. What does one have to do to please the manager?

The importance of knowing what your manager thinks of your performance is tied directly to the manager's heavy influence on one's job security. The manager's dissatisfaction with performance will quite likely lead to adverse actions. Examples of such actions occur periodically in the organization. Farewell parties provide mute testimony of the final outcome of dissatisfaction.

Individuals prefer not to get a sudden shock. If dissatisfaction exists and one knows about it, remedial steps might change things. So it is that this type of knowledge is of critical importance to every subordinate. The importance seems to be true at all levels of the organization.

Recognition of the importance of knowing what one's manager thinks of one's performance has led most organizations to have some type of performance appraisal program. Just how well do managers provide knowledge of performance to subordinates?

Consider the following survey data:

How well do you know what your superior thinks of performance?	Five percent say they don't know. Thirty-five percent say they have some idea. Sixty percent say they have a "good idea" or a "very very definite idea."

This data suggests there is room for improvement in the current level of effectiveness with which managers provide knowledge of how they view performance. This widespread condition is one reason for devoting Part III of this book to the performance interview. It is our hope that managers will (1) improve their skill and, then (2) apply the skill. This would mean fulfilling the vital requirement of informing subordinates about their performance.

Receiving Information about What Is Going on in One's Organization. Many an organization has a problem. They refer to it as a "communications" problem. It usually has to do with personnel reacting to an absence of information about what is going on. Several types of information are of consequence here. They are reflected by the following questions:

1. How well are we achieving our goals?
2. How well are we doing compared to competition?
3. How well are others doing whose performance affects our performance?
4. What difficulties exist, what problems exist which impact on our success?

Why is this type of information important to an individual? For three reasons. First, the information enables the individual to contribute more effectively. Second, the information tells the subordinate that he or she is considered important enough to be kept informed. Third, the regular provision of news, both good and bad, says the organization is willing to communicate.

How well are executives doing in providing this type of data? Our data says it is highly variable. Some organizations do very well, some do not.

Consider the following results:

		Percent Saying "Satisfied" or "Well Satisfied"*	
	Average Organization	Best Organization	Poorest Organization
1. How satisfied are you with the information you receive about what is going on in the overall organization?	76	88	61

* These results are from 30 different organizations varying in size from 20 to 500 managers. Average number of managers was 86. The "best" organizations are the top seven, the "poorest" organizations are the bottom seven.

Advance Knowledge of Changes That May Affect the Subordinate.   There are many changes which affect an individual. Among them are:

1. Working hours.
2. Working schedules.
3. Working rules.
4. Changes in salary.
5. Changes in one's superior.
6. Change in location.
7. Change in one's position.
8. Change in one's working companions.
9. Change in one's employment.
10. Any change which affects one's status.

The list could be extended. One might more easily identify what can be changed without it affecting or upsetting somebody.

Why is advance knowledge of change so important? It is important for several reasons. A sense of fair play says you don't suddenly surprise somebody, particularly if the change is an adverse one. Secondly, the way changes are handled tells individuals in an organization whether they are respected and appreciated. Third, cooperation of individuals in making a change successful is often required. Advance information, plus other participative processes, help in getting this cooperation.

How well do executives do in providing this type of information? Unfortunately, we haven't covered this area in our surveys. Our casual observation leads us to conclude that there is extreme variation. Some managers and some organizations do a real good job. Some do a very poor job.

Knowledge of Organizational "Environmental" Factors. Organizational "environmental" factors are many and varied. They include traditions, myths, sentiments, taboos, rituals, rules, regulations, policies, and protocol. The organization which is reknown for stressing environmental factors is the Marine Corps. Their sheer smallness has increased the importance of these factors. Few business and individual organizations have such well-established environmental factors as the Marine Corps.

Some organizations, however, are well known for having a distinct "culture." One would put such companies as IBM, Ford, and Revlon in this category. They are heavily influenced by the founder and his successors in each instance.

Why is knowledge of environmental factors important? First, one's advancement and even job security is influenced for better or for worse by one's observance and compliance with "environmental" factors. This happens quite apart from one's performance on a job.

Second, the ability to get things done, or even to attempt to do a given thing, may be heavily impacted by environmental factors. Obviously, the higher one goes in an organization the more consequential this type of knowledge becomes. Some organizations have included "orientation" in these cultural factors in their management education courses. In this instance, we have no survey data on how organizations actually provide such knowledge.

We see environment factors having a potential for either a positive or a negative impact upon performance. We would suggest it might well be worth identifying the dominant factors. One could then measure whether they are positive or negative in their impact.

Knowledge of the Personal "Peculiarities" of the Immediate Superior. Personal peculiarities are multitudinous. Does the boss want everything reduced to one page? Does the boss prefer to avoid conflict? Does he or she make decisions in the morning? Is the superior conceptual? Is the superior concerned about people? What are his or her more basic values? These and many other similar questions can be considered as personal peculiarities. One might be alert to the peculiarities which occur most often and have a bearing on the immediate work situation.

McGregor was very insightful in isolating this type of knowledge out as of real consequence. I have often used a term "comfort index" to describe this phenomena. All superiors have a comfort index. It is smart for a subordinate to recognize what contributes to the comfort index and then program to keep the index at or above the needed level.

Satisfaction of one's own needs can be directly affected by knowledge of the superior's peculiarities. This is one type of knowledge the subordinate should take the initiative in ferreting out.

We have now considered seven types of information of direct concern to providing the needed sense of security for subordinates. Let's now turn to a third condition, consistent discipline.

Consistent Discipline

The third requirement for providing a subordinate with a sense of security is that of consistent discipline. It must take the form of positive support for "right" actions, as well as criticism and punishment for "wrong" ones. Subordinates, in order to be secure, require consistent discipline in both senses.

They require, first of all, the strong and willing backing of their superiors for those actions which are in accord with what is expected of them. There is much talk among some managements about superiors who fail to "back up" their subordinates. The insecurity that arises when subordinates do not know under what conditions they will be backed up leads them to "keep their necks pulled in" at all times. Buck-passing and its consequent frictions and resentment are inevitable under such circumstances.

Given a clear knowledge of what is expected of them, subordinates require, in addition, the definite assurance that they will have the unqualified support of their superiors so long as their actions are consistent with policies and are taken within the limits of one's responsibility. Only then can they have the security and confidence that will enable them to take initiative, to strive to do their jobs well.

At the same time the subordinates must know that failure to live up to their responsibilities, or to observe the rules which are established, will result in punishment. Every individual has many personal needs which conflict with the demands of the job. If they know that breaking the rules or indulging oneself to satisfy these needs will almost inevitably result in the frustration of their vital long-range needs, self-discipline will more likely occur.

What frequently happens is this. The superior, in trying to

be a "good fellow," fails to maintain discipline and to obtain adherence to the standards of performance which are necessary. Subordinates, being human beings striving to satisfy their needs, "take advantage of the situation." The superior then begins to disapprove of the subordinates, in spite of the fact that he or she is to blame for their behavior. Perhaps the superior "cracks down" on them; perhaps he or she simply grows more and more critical and disapproving. In either event, because the superior has failed to establish consistent discipline, in an atmosphere of genuine approval, subordinates are threatened. This leads quite directly to antagonism and, therefore, to further actions of which the superior disapproves. Thus a viscious circle of disapproval—antagonistic acts—more disapproval—more antagonistic acts is set up. In the end it becomes extremely difficult to remedy a situation of this kind because both superior and subordinate have a chip-on-the-shoulder attitude which must be abolished before the relationship can improve.

What is the prevailing practice of executives with regard to consistent discipline? Coaching survey results from several thousand managers and executives provide the following data:

1. If an immediate subordinates does not achieve the expected results, how likely is your superior to express criticism?

   Sixty percent report this happens in "most cases" or in "all such cases."

2. If an immediate subordinates achieves a significant result, how likely is your superior to praise this individual

   Sixty-five percent report this happens in "most cases" or in "all such cases."

3. If the performance of an immediate subordinates is not sustained at a satisfactory level, how likely is your superior to take some appropriate action?

   Sixty-three percent say it happens more often than not, or in all cases.

4. Based upon the results you have secured over the last several years, do you feel you have been accorded the recognition by your superior which you deserve?	Seventy-one percent say this has happened with "almost no exception," or is "almost always received."
5. How often, when your superior's support would be helpful to you, does your superior provide it?	Seventy-four percent say this is "frequently," or "almost always" done.

Looking at the data, from a positive viewpoint it appears that a majority get the benefit of consistent discipline. However, about one third or one fourth evidently do not. The reader can make assumptions as to the way his or her subordinates would answer the above questions.

Subordinates, then, require the security of knowing that they can count on the firm support of their superiors for doing what is "right" and firm pressure, even punishment, to prevent them doing what is "wrong." *But this discipline must be established and maintained in an atmosphere of approval.* Otherwise, the subordinates' suspicion and resentment of their superiors will lead to the opposite reaction from the desired one. A mild degree of discipline is sufficient in an atmosphere of approval; even the most severe discipline will, in the end, be unsuccessful in an atmosphere of disapproval.

This twofold emphasis is McGregor's great contribution. The entire process for the counseling interview will be based upon empathy and standards, which is analogous to McGregor's stress on atmosphere of approval and consistent discipline.

Needed Position

The previous three requirements have stressed the interrelationship between a superior and a subordinate. The superior provides an atmosphere of approval, a variety of critical types of knowledge, and consistent discipline. We would now stress the importance of the position occupied by the subordinate. For a real sense of security, the occupant of a position must be in a position which is needed. The working relationship between superior and subordinate may be fine, but it doesn't last unless the position of the subordinate is an enduring one.

An experience with a recession dramatizes the important relationship between a sense of security and a position which is vitally needed. Popular journals frequently carry articles about how an individual feels to be suddenly unemployed. This requirement is influenced by the way you set up and change your organization. Every position must be fully justified from the very beginning. In this dynamic era, it is natural that some positions will increase in importance and some will decrease. Some will become unnecessary. However, the more rigorously positions are justified from the very beginning, the better.

In the career discussion part of this book we will consider a process pertaining to the abolition of positions and resulting discussions to be held with incumbents.

Organizational Success

Have you ever been a part of a company or subdivision that was marginal? Did it go bankrupt? A real sense of security requires more than an effective working relationship with a superior and a needed position. It requires that the organization in which one finds himself or herself will be successful or have a good chance to become so.

Some industries have great stability. Others have little or none. Some companies are extremely stable, others are extremely volatile. No matter what the pattern is in your own situation, the importance of the need for continued organizational success needs to be recognized.

We mentioned earlier that certain knowledge was very vital. Knowledge of the odds of success or lack of success of the organization represents an additional type of knowledge which directly impacts upon one's sense of security. Certainly any significant change in the contemplated success of an organization needs to be communicated.

Each of the executive interviews considered in this book is designed to contribute to the performance needed to get the results required for success. While the interview contribution can be consequential, many other factors beyond the scope of this book also impinge on the success of the enterprise.

The Necessity for Independence

When the subordinates have achieved a reasonable degree of genuine security in their relationship with their superiors, in their position and in their organization, they will begin to seek ways of utilizing more fully their capacities and skills, of achieving through their own efforts a larger degree of satisfaction from their work. Given security, the subordinates seek to develop themselves. This active search for independence is constructive and healthy. It is collaborative and friendly, yet genuinely self-assertive.

If, on the other hand, the subordinates feel their dependence on their superiors is extreme, and if they lack security for other reasons, they will fight, ineffectively, for freedom. This reactive struggle for independence is founded on fear and distrust. It leads to friction and strife, and it tends to perpetuate itself because it interferes with the development of an atmosphere of approval which is essential to security.

McGregor suggests that these two fundamentally opposite ways in which subordinates seek to acquire independence have entirely different consequences. Since we are concerned with the conditions of the successful subordinate/superior relationship, we shall emphasize the active way rather than the reactive way of striving for independence.

CONDITIONS NEEDED TO SHIFT FROM DEPENDENCY TO INDEPENDENCE

One might say that the foundations of security have been laid by those conditions which counteract the dependent position of the subordinate. What conditions are needed to shift from dependency to independence? I would suggest there are five:

1. Self-measurement.
2. Involvement.
3. Responsibility.
4. Opportunity for a hearing.
5. Supportive overall climate.

Let's consider each of these five conditions.

Self-Measurement

What is meant by self-measurement? Self-measurement means the individual has a basis for determining success and failure with regard to performance in a given position. Preferably, the individual has a set of end results against which to measure. End results or outcomes are quite different from activities and tasks. We will be suggesting one real value of working against goals is that options on alternate ways are kept open. Ideally, a subordinate has a goals document representing his or her commitments to achieve certain end results.

Looking at the document periodically results in a feeling of pride or a sense of guilt or anxiety. However, the guilt or anxiety is not in personal terms re a happy or unhappy superior. It is in operational terms, focused on end results. A problem-solving approach to a negative variance from established outcome provides an operational way of reacting.

The great popularity of management by objectives efforts over the last ten years attest to a widespread recognition of the importance of an individual being committed to achieving certain end results. However, not all MBO programs are successful. Further, many MBO programs do not stress self-measurement, but the sustained popularity of MBO efforts suggest they are contributing to this requirement.

The scope of this book does not permit providing detailed suggestions on how to get an objectives effort to contribute to meeting this self-measurement requirement. The bibliography for this chapter will provide references for those who wish to explore MBO further.

Involvement

Involvement can be narrow or broad. In the superior/subordinate relationship involvement can concentrate on involvement when decisions are made which affect a subordinate or decisions are made upon which subordinates can make a contribution. One of the most important conditions of subordinates' growth and development centers around their opportunity to express their ideas and to contribute suggestions before their superiors take action on matters which involve them. Through participation of this kind, subordinates become more and more aware of their superiors' problems, and they obtain a genuine satisfaction in knowing that their opinions and ideas are given consideration in the search for solutions.

Participation is of consequence at all levels of an organization. The important point is that participation cannot be successful unless the conditions of security are adequately met. Many failures of participation efforts can be traced directly to this fundamental fact that active independence cannot be achieved in the absence of adequate security.

How often do executives provide this opportunity for involvement? Again, we do not have data to permit generalizing to all executives. However, data from a sample of 200 executives in 25 quite diverse organizations does provide some data pertaining to prevailing practice.

1. Innovative thinking, creative ideas, and new ways of approaching problems are encouraged in our organization.	Seventy-five percent say this is "quite" or "entirely" characteristic.
2. My manager is receptive to new ideas and suggestions for change.	Eighty-eight percent say this is done in a satisfactory manner.
3. In establishment of things you are expected to accomplish, how often does your superior do it with little contribution from you?	Thirty-three percent say this is what usually happens.
4. When discussing problems and undertakings, does your superior endeavor to understand your viewpoint?	Sixty percent say this does happen regularly.
5. How often does your superior evidence an interest when you express an opinion or make a suggestion on an important subject?	Sixty percent say this does happen regularly.

The above results, as reflected in these selected questions, suggest a rather consistent pattern. Opportunity for involvement seems to be provided by executives about two thirds of the time. As one would expect, the pattern varies widely for different superiors. Admittedly, the data reflects subordinates' viewpoints. This may not be an entirely accurate reflection of the true situation. Each executive will have to think through the extent of involvement which prevails and that which is appropriate.

There is a real challenge and a deep satisfaction for the subordinate who is given the opportunity to aid in the solution of the difficult but fascinating problems that arise frequently in any business or industrial organization. Superiors who, having provided security for their subordinates, encourage them to accept the challenge represented by involvement are almost invariably surprised at the fruitfulness of the results. The chief executive of one company remarked, after a few management conferences designed to encourage this kind of participation, that he had never before realized in considering his problems how many alternative possibilities were available, nor how inadequate had been the knowledge upon which he based his decisions.

Responsibility

There are two aspects to authority. One is to grant responsibility; the other is to encourage subordinates to accept responsibility. Granting responsibility sometimes is referred to as delegating. Some executives are quite skillful in shifting responsibility in small amounts and doing so at periodic intervals. Let's assume that the superior does take the initiative to delegate. It does not follow immediately that a subordinate will fully accept the newly granted authority.

McGregor stresses that a corollary of the desire for participation is a desire for responsibility. It is another manifestation of the active search for independence. Insecure or rebellious subordinates, seeking independence in the reactive sense, do not accept responsibility. They are seeking protection, not the opportunity for self-realization and development.

The willingness to assume responsibility is a genuine maturational phenomenon. Subordinates cannot accept responsibility until they have achieved a certain degree of emotional security in their relationship with their superiors. Then they want responsibility. They accept it with obvious pleasure and pride. And if responsibility is given to them gradually so that they are not suddenly made insecure again by too great a load of it, they will continue to accept more and more.

What data do we have on the extent to which superiors do grant authority or grant responsibility? Again, we have data from the limited population we have mentioned before. The results from questions pertinent to the issue of responsibility follow. Admittedly, the data is the view as seen by the subordinate.

1. How fully would you say your superior delegates?	Seventy-seven percent say the superior "does so" or "does so with only a few exceptions."
2. How well do you know what your authority is in carrying out your responsibilities?	Sixty-four percent say they "definitely know what their authority is," or "know, with only a few exceptions."
3. Has your superior advised you of the limitations to be observed by you in making your decisions?	Sixty-seven percent say this has "not been done," or "has been done in very general terms."

If one looks for the formality represented by the third question, the results are amazingly low. The "opinion" or "attitude" toward the satisfactoriness of delegation, from the subordinate's viewpoint, shows that somewhat over two thirds do feel satisfied.

The process of granting responsibility to subordinates is a

delicate one. There are vast individual differences in tolerance for the inevitable pressures and insecurities attendant upon the acceptance of responsibility. Some subordinates seem to be content to achieve a high degree of security without independence. Others thrive on the risks and the dangers of being "on their own." However, there are few subordinates whose capabilities in this direction are fully realized. It is unwise to attribute the absence of a desire for responsibility to the individual's personality alone until one has made certain that the relationship to superiors is genuinely secure.

Opportunity for a Hearing

McGregor uses the term "right to appeal." We prefer to say "opportunity for a hearing." Both phrases imply that a recourse is available to a subordinate when he or she sincerely differs with a superior. You may recall a situation when you felt you were "betting your job" or "putting your job on the line." In some instances the difference may have to do with a business or operational issue. In other instances it may be a personal issue, such as one's salary, incentive payment, or advancement.

Why is an opportunity for a hearing so important? The existence of a difference between a superior and a subordinate makes the subordinate acutely aware that he or she is dependent upon the superior. The chance for the subordinate to "win" is low. The chance for the subordinate to feel helpless is great. In fact, how such differences are handled is an acid test of the extent of dependency required of a subordinate.

If a subordinate must always defer to a superior's position, the opportunity to gain independence or self-sufficiency is low. As likely as not, the interaction will become a reactive struggle. This may be manifested by a loss of interest in contributing; a lack of willingness to argue; a pattern of minimum investment; adherence to a "low-profile," "don't-rock-your-boat" pattern of behavior. These consequences suggest that it is important to provide an opportunity for a hearing.

A superior has a straightforward approach to this requirement. Let's assume you are faced with a sincere difference of opinion with a subordinate. It is apparent that the difference can't be resolved. Therefore, you not only suggest but encourage the subordinate to talk over the issue with your superior. In addition, you advise your superior of the issue and ask that your subordinate be accorded an audience.

Our surveys have not covered this requirement so we do not have data on prevailing practice. We have not heard of any formal or announced hearing program in any company. However, we have observed some companies where a hearing can occur with little difficulty. In other companies, a hearing would be an impossibility.

If the relationship between subordinate and superior is a successful one, the opportunity for a hearing will rarely be exercised. Nevertheless, the awareness that a hearing is possible, if needed, provides the subordinate with a feeling of independence which is not otherwise possible.

Supportive Overall Climate

What is meant by "supportive overall climate"? We are referring to the climate which prevails at two or more levels above a given executive. The word "climate" refers to such factors as the reward and penalty system, the nature of communication processes, and the importance attached to human resources. The term "supportive" refers to the existence of a climate which contributes to positive superior/subordinate relationships.

The importance of such a supportive overall climate is really apparent. Let's assume an individual executive sincerely attempts to implement the previously suggested requirements. However, the prevailing climate prevents or interferes with the implementation process. In some instances the actions may be taken anyhow. This sometimes is referred to as "bootlegging." In other instances the executive "erects an umbrella" to protect his or her subordinates. In some instances the climate may make it impossible to avoid the fear of capricious or unpredictable negative decisions. Thus it is that climate can either be a real assist or a real deterrent to the provision of the requirements we have been discussing.

Suggestions on changing the overall climate of an organization are beyond the scope of this book. Several references are provided in the bibliography to fulfill this need.

SUMMARY

Subordinates in a business or industrial organization are dependent for the satisfaction of many of their vital needs upon the behavior and attitudes of their superiors. They require, therefore, a feeling of confidence that they can satisfy their needs if they do what is expected of them. Given this security, they then require opportunities for self-realization and development.

Among the conditions influencing the subordinates' feelings of security are: (1) an atmosphere of approval; (2) numerous types of knowledge; (3) consistent discipline, both in the form of backing when subordinates are "right" and in the form of punishment when they are "wrong"; (4) having a position which is needed; (5) being in an organization which is successful; and (6) the need for independence.

The conditions under which subordinates can realize their

own potentialities and become independent include: (1) an adequate basis for self-measurement, (2) opportunities for involvement in the solution of problems and in the discussion of actions which may affect them, (3) the opportunity to assume responsibility as they become ready for it, (4) the opportunity . for a hearing, and (5) a supportive overall climate.

These conditions are basic. Upon their fulfillment rests the success or failure of the subordinate/superior relationship at each level of an organization.

It has become apparent in this chapter that one's position is of great consequence. In the following chapter attention will be given to the importance of a position to an individual. Again, the behavior research contribution here is voluminous so we will need to select those contributions which are immediately relevant to the types of executive interviewing under consideration.

2

The Importance of a
Position to an Individual

FIVE TYPES of interviews are considered in this book. Each type relates to an individual and a position. The selection interview involves a position to be filled. An individual must be selected who can secure the results expected of an individual in such a position. The performance interview concerns the performance of an individual in a position. The counseling interview has to do with a behavior which is inappropriate for an individual in a position in a given organization. The career discussion relates to future positions of concern to an individual. Finally, the removal interview involves the need to remove an individual from a position.

One's skill in these five types of interviews will be enhanced by a better understanding of the importance of a position to an individual. Some idea of the importance of a position to an individual is revealed by the rated level of importance. In study after study of individuals in managerial and professional positions, 100 percent say: "Having interesting work to do" is important. In fact, when considering the response "very important," one's position is practically always ranked number one over all other morale or job satisfaction factors in our extensive managerial surveys. The im-

portance of a position to an individual will be explored
further as we consider the following:

1. The meaning of work.
2. One's self-concept in relation to a position.
3. The special values of an executive's position.

THE MEANING OF WORK

Let's give consideration to the meaning of holding a position to an individual. Numerous studies have been made of
the meaning of work. Such studies identify many benefits individuals derive from work, in addition to that of economic
necessity. Frequently mentioned benefits include the following:

1. Something to do and think about, a routine.
2. Association and friendship.
3. Purposeful activity, a sense of accomplishment, the satis-
    faction of problem solving.
4. Self-respect, a feeling of personal worth.
5. Recognition from others, a source of prestige.
6. Creativity or intrinsic enjoyment of the work.
7. Opportunity to be of service to others.

Ann Roe[1] has studied the psychology of occupations. She uses
the term occupation much as we do the term position. She
contends that:* "In our society there is no single situation
that is, potentially, so capable of giving some satisfactions at
all levels of basic needs as is the occupation." She refers to
Maslow's[2] list of basic needs:

---

* See bibliography for details on each reference.

1. The psychological needs.
2. The safety needs.
3. The need for belongingness and love.
4. The need for importance, respect, self-esteem, independence.
5. The need for information.
6. The need for understanding.
7. The need for beauty.
8. The need for self-actualization.

Roe stresses the economic value of an occupation for physiological and safety needs. An occupation also contributes directly to the need for belonging. The importance of an occupation in meeting the need for esteem is obvious. Feelings of personal esteem are closely linked to the amount of responsibility and the degree of freedom one's position entails. There is an opportunity to get one's need for information and understanding at least partially fulfilled in one's position. This, of course, depends greatly upon the nature of the superior/subordinate relationship discussed in the prior chapter. The opportunity to have one's need for self-actualization met is also directly related to one's position. Roe didn't note any relationship between one's position and the need for beauty.

Studs Terkel[3] wrote a book entitled, *Working*. It consisted of interviews with individuals from all walks of life. As a reporter, he just gave a verbatim report of the interviews. No editorializing. No generalizations. However, you can't read a dozen interviews without seeing trends. A reading of seven interviews of executives revealed a real compulsion on their part to work. Quotes from these interviews follow.
Quote from a TV/radio executive:

Ours is a twenty-four hour-a-day business. . . . I am on a seven-day-a-week job and I love it.

Quote from a factory owner:

All night long I think about this place. I love my work. It isn't the money. It's just a way of expressing my feelings.

Quote from a consultant:

There's one corporation chief I know who worked, conservatively, nineteen, twenty hours a day. His whole life was his business.

Quote from an executive:

In my climb to get to the top of the corporation, money was secondary. . . It's the power, the status, the prestige. Frankly, it's delightful to be at the top and have everybody calling you Mr. Ross and have a plane at your disposal and a car and a driver at your disposal.

Quote from a young business owner:

My initial interest was in making money. Later, business became a game. Money is the kind of way you keep score. How else you gonna see yourself go up? . . . you get your thrill out of seeing the business grow. Just building it bigger and bigger. . . I guess people get different thrills out of business in different ways. There's a lot of satisfaction in showing up people who thought you'd never amount to anything.

Quote from a director of a bakery:

Work is an essential part of being alive. Your work is your identity. It tells you who you are. It's gotten so abstract. People don't work for the sake of working. They are working for a car, a new house or a vacation. It's not the work itself that's important to them. There's such a joy in doing work well.

Quote from a football coach:

If you enjoy your job, it isn't work, it's fun . . . when you
get so engrossed in your job during the season it has to come
ahead of your family.

Work addiction is a phrase which comes to mind as you
read these excerpts. Most of the executives feared retirement.
They were proving themselves, testing themselves, validating
themselves. Achievement and accomplishment were the measures they used.

Work can be viewed as an opportunity for individual self-
validation. By self-validation I mean confirmation of the existence and worth of one's self. You are convinced you exist
and are worthwhile by evidence that you affect somebody or
something. The interactions present in a work environment
offer many opportunities for self-validation.

We must understand the full significance of work to human
identity when it is organized as jobs or positions performed
to make a living. Its importance is dramatically revealed
when an individual is faced with prolonged unemployment.
The shock is great. The individual feels humiliated. To the
question of "What is the most important thing in life," the
unemployed are likely to say "work" because with nothing to
do you can't enjoy anything!

A position, particularly in the hierarchy of management,
provides an individual with a major and sustained opportunity to influence. The "feedback" thus derived provides the
basis for continuous self-validation.

ONE'S SELF-CONCEPT IN RELATION TO A POSITION

The importance of work to an individual can be better understood if we relate work to one's self-concept. Understanding the nature and degree of the individual's self-concept
helps to understand an individual psychologically. An in-

dividual's self-concept is the single most significant key to the individual's behavior. So intensely does an individual feel the need of a positive view about himself or herself that he or she may go to any lengths to avoid coming face to face with facts which place the self-concept in jeopardy.

The following may be stated about our self-concept:

1. One's self-concept has two interrelated aspects: it entails a sense of personal efficacy or self-confidence, and a sense of personal worth or self-respect.

2. One's self-concept is not a value which, once achieved, is maintained effortlessly and automatically thereafter. Continuous action is needed not only to gain it but also to keep it.

3. One's self-concept is deeply influenced by one's progress in his or her career. A career consists of a hierarchy or ladder of opportunities of increasing importance. To climb the ladder, rung after rung, in competition with others, directly impacts one's self-esteem.

Gellerman[4] devotes a chapter to the concept of self in his book, *Productivity and Motivation.* He stresses the following:

> Ideas about oneself are shaped by reference to people. The self concept is really a social concept. The self concept is made up of a sense of competence and a sense of self worth. The individual's self concept, which he or she brings to the job, is an amalgam of many things—parents' and peers' reactions, one's record of successes and failures, and one's notion of the rewards which are deserved.

Gellerman makes three basic statements about one's self concept:

> First, any individual has some fairly persistent ideas— usually too vague to be articulated—about what kind of person he is. This is his self concept. He tries at all times to behave

as much like the kind of person he thinks he is as his environment permits. When his environment restricts him from acting
in ways he considers appropriate for himself, he will feel
frustrated and will cooperate only as much as he must. His
instinct, no matter how strongly his environment suppresses it,
is always to be himself.

Second, the individual's understanding of the environment
he lives in does not necessarily correspond to the ideas of other
people living in the same "objective" environment. He draws
most of his conclusions about the kind of world he is living in
long before he has access to all the facts, or even the judgment
to weigh the facts, and he seldom revises or even questions
his assumptions about the world. As far as he is concerned, the
world has certain constraints and certain opportunities built
into it for him and he is unlikely to try to escape from these
self-imposed boundaries regardless of whether anyone else
thinks they are there.

Third, any individual is likely to conduct himself, most of
the time, in such a way as to enhance the likelihood of being
able to be himself in the kind of environment he thinks he is
living in. This strategy is what we have called his psychological
advantage. It may vary all the way from exuberantly seizing
opportunities to passively making peace with the lack of them,
but in every case it represents what the individual thinks is the
optimum compromise between what he wants to be and what
the world is likely to permit him to be.

One's self-concept is enhanced by a feeling of being successful. Let me suggest that there are five things which make
you feel successful. Endeavor to recall recent situations in
which you felt quite successful. Check those situations with
these five basic situations. You will feel successful when—

1. You receive praise from someone you respect.
2. You secure a reward you consider important.
3. You are part of a successful group that is accomplishing
    something.

4.   You are making personal progress in your chosen occupation.

5.   You have mastered a given field of endeavor. You are recognized as an "authority" or helpful resource.

An explanation of each of these five basic situations is in order.

Praise from Someone You Respect

The source of praise and the nature of praise are both consequential. To give a feeling of success, the source of praise must be someone who is respected. "Well done" from someone who is experienced, who is knowledgeable, who is an expert, really means something. It is interesting to observe highly technical individuals. They often respect peers more than they do a superior. Hence, praise or approbation from a peer really counts with them.

Respect isn't an all inclusive thing. A superior might be respected because he or she knows the industry, is strong technically, is an effective manager, or is a nice individual. Earning respect has been and still is often more difficult for a woman than a man. Fortunately this is slowly changing in today's business world.

The nature of praise is also important. Is the statement genuine or does it have a phony ring? Is it heartfelt or taken from a recent reading of a Dale Carnegie–type book? Is the praise for an expected result or for some means which was utilized? Is praise provided for initiative or for conformity?

The importance of praise is best illustrated by your own remembrance of meaningful praise received. Think back over your experience. When did you receive praise which you still vividly remember? As often as not, individuals go back in their memories for five or even ten years. This vivid recall says something about the importance of praise. It also says something about the rareness of receiving genuine praise.

Periodically, throughout performance, counseling, and career discussions, we will be encouraging you to give attention to motivational issues. This is a means of providing some of the conditions, such as praise, which enhance a person's self-concept and reinforce effective behavior.

Rewards Considered Important

This basic situation is a most fascinating one. It is one we overlook quite frequently. Each of us has a tendency to assume others attach the same importance as we do to a reward. Some executives are shocked when a subordinate refuses a promotion. They prize such a reward, why shouldn't the subordinate? Let's assume you are conducting an employment interview. Obviously, selecting the right individual is a prime objective of yours. It becomes critical to know just what factors are important to the prospective employee. Is it the reward, the challenge, the status, the power? Is it the avoidance of commuting or the fulfilling of responsibilities to the family? There is an endless variety of reasons an individual would consider an offered position in a positive light.

During performance and counseling interviews a variance exists which you want to see changed. However, what is in it for the subordinate to change? What are the possible rewards? Which ones are really important to the subordinate? Insight into the answers to these two questions will be of real assistance to conducting a productive interview. A career discussion is often conducted because a subordinate is concerned about one reward, namely advancement. The entire career discussion, in effect, has to do with the issue of jointly endeavoring to secure a prized result, namely advancement.

Part of a Successful Group

Let's look at sports for a minute. Some teams win regularly. Some lose regularly. What a difference there is in the interactions and behaviors during the game, in the locker room, during practice sessions, and, even, at home. It takes a different managing approach when your team is losing.

Now consider your present situation. If you are a part of a successful group, this certainly enhances your self-concept. If your present group isn't successful this certainly impacts your own self-concept.

In a prior chapter stress was placed upon the importance of certain kinds of knowledge. Knowing your peers' objectives, knowing your bosses' objectives and being kept up-to-date on their success in achieving their objectives is directly related to this basic condition. It is a rare individual who doesn't feel a strong need to be part of a group, a group which is successful.

Personal Progress in Your Chosen Occupation

Progress in one's chosen field of endeavor is manifested in many different ways. Within a hierarchial organization, promotion to increasing higher level positions provides a dramatic example of progress. Interestingly, some individuals have a well-worked-out time schedule of when they should arrive at given levels. Others measure their progress against their peers, while some compete against their college classmates.

A perplexity for many recently married couples occurs

when both work. Who makes progress faster? Some individuals refuse to move unless their spouse can also benefit from the move. The feeling of making progress in one's chosen career implies moving through a series of positions, usually in a hierarchial arrangement.

Mastering a Chosen Field

Mastering a chosen field means you have reached a stage where you are recognized as an "authority," a helpful resource. This recognition can occur at any level of an organization. More likely than not, this stage is reached after considerable experience.

Summary

Let's suppose you are in a position in which you perform in a most satisfactory manner. You are likely to receive praise. At least you are eligible for it. You are likely to get a reward, or at least earn consideration for a reward. You feel you are helping the group succeed and getting satisfaction out of doing this. As you move from a lower to a higher position you feel you are making progress. Upon having performed satisfactorily in a position for some time, you get to a point of having mastered your chosen field of endeavor. You are gaining the benefit of most of the ways of feeling successful.

But now suppose the Peter Principle has come into play. To be safe, let's say you are two levels above your level of competence. The Peter Principle then becomes most apparent. The situation becomes tragic. You immediately lose all five conditions which make you feel successful and enhance your self-esteem.

You are also vulnerable to trauma when your position isn't

really needed. However, this doesn't present as shattering a shock as being judged unsatisfactory or inadequate. It means a dislocation, but it doesn't shatter one's self-concept.

Let's now consider the special significance of an executive position.

SPECIAL VALUES OF AN EXECUTIVE POSITION

An executive position has the potential of fulfilling many needs of an executive. *Status* is a value of concern to many executives. It almost borders on the ludicrous, at times, to see executives strive to get their status needs filled by positions with highly prized titles. A position often provides a source of *power* which meets the need of some executives to wield power and to avoid being subservient to another powerful individual. Reaching a given position often means one has bested one's competition. Some executives are extremely competitive. The "footrace" is exhilarating, especially when one wins. Notice how frequently an executive resigns when a competitor has been given a top position.

There is another powerful value of an executive position. It has to do with timely *feedback*. One secures data quickly which can be interpreted readily in terms of success or failure. This quick feedback is adrenalin to many an executive. In fact, after a week on vacation, the absence of this feedback amounts to deprivation for the executive who is a "work alcoholic."

Many an executive finds a position fulfills a need to pit his or her intellect against a series of everchanging problems and opportunities. Some executives, upon moving from a larger enterprise to a smaller one, feel the loss of intellectual challenge because of the decreased complexity. They usually express it as being bored.

The executive position, for many, permits one to make a contribution to society, to be of service. Not all executives, of course, have this need. Finally, the executive position does fulfill an economic need to live at a certain standard of living.

It is appropriate to consider that an executive position, in fulfilling the above needs, is a means of self-validation. It is a means of confirming one's self-concept, of reassuring one's self-esteem. No wonder some wives of executives complain that their husband's job is "his mistress."

Let's relate this discussion to the previous chapter. Unless one works entirely alone, he or she will be in a position in a hierarchy. This means one is likely to have a superior and, probably, subordinates.

The previous chapter suggested that a superior needs to provide the conditions which make for a sense of security. This permits subordinates to become actively independent. This is another way of saying they have a direct and personal opportunity of getting many benefits from their position. It becomes a matter of performance and not politics!

3

Satisfactory Performance

LET'S SUPPOSE we add to our skills in several types of interviewing. Let's further assume we apply the skills we have learned. What evidence do we have of our effectiveness? The real evidence will be satisfactory performance. A selection interview is successful if it results in the choice of an individual who goes on to achieve the results expected of the individual in the position. Once an interviewer called a recent appointee into his office and said, "When I first hired you some months ago, you told me how good you were. Would you mind repeating your statements, I'm beginning to get discouraged."

Certainly the most beneficial consequence of a performance interview is an improvement in performance, preferably reaching a satisfactory level or better. A counseling interview is aimed at changing behavior or performance which is quite at variance with established or generally accepted rules.

The critical feature in career discussions is to aspire to a position which one will likely perform quite satisfactorily. The removal interview admits that an individual did not reach a satisfactory level of performance and removal became a necessity.

In this chapter we will give attention to factors which impact upon satisfactory performance. Again these factors will stand you in good stead as you experiment with the new mechanics of interviewing. They should assist you in combining the right dynamics with the right mechanics. This is essential when dealing with complex human beings. The factors to be included are:

1. A helpful performance "formula."
2. Requirements for getting a change in habits.
3. The use of both positive and negative motivation.
4. Environmental or climate factors.
5. The pygmalion effect.
6. Individuals visualized as energy packages.

A HELPFUL PERFORMANCE "FORMULA"

Over a period of years I have found the following rather simple formula to be of help as I plan and conduct interviews.

$$\text{Ability} \times \text{Willingness} = \text{Performance}$$

Ability has several facets. It includes knowledge, skill, and experience. Willingness refers primarily to an attitude. It may be positive or negative. Willingness is positive when there is a desire to accomplish the expected performance. There is a concern, a commitment, maybe even an enthusiasm to perform. The lack of willingness would certainly add up to a negative situation.

This formula applies to the selection interview. As likely as not, you will have two or more candidates to consider. As you make your comparisons you will endeavor to identify the individual who is most able. Then you will need to look at the willingness or motivation factor. One individual may be most enthusiastic about the new position. Another may not be interested in the position. In your experience you have probably noticed that individuals with modest ability but great willingness often perform quite satisfactorily. You have also noted that high ability and low willingness usually leads to unsatisfactory performance. Let's now consider how the formula applies to the performance interview.

Assume that a variance between expected performance and actual performance exists for a given individual who works for you. You have to find out whether the variance is due to ability factors or to willingness factors. Possibly both factors may be influencing the variance. If your analysis leads you to believe that ability factors are predominant, certain types of remedial action will be appropriate. If willingness factors predominate, other quite different actions would be appropriate.

Ability factors may be personal, such as lack of skill, lack of knowledge, or lack of experience. They may be situational, such as lack of performance by another department, a breakdown in equipment, or adverse working conditions.

Willingness factors may be individual, such as personal problems outside work, attitude toward supervisor, or attitude toward work. Subsequently, we will suggest exploring causes before planning action in a performance interview. The main reason for suggesting that causes for variances be explored during performance interviews relates to this formula. You have to get a fix on the predominant reason or reasons for a variance before you can plan effective remedial action.

The formula also helps in planning one's counseling interview. An individual manifests a behavior which is deemed inappropriate. Your purpose in the counseling process is to assist the individual in changing. You will be asking yourself questions such as the following: Can the individual change? Will the individual make the effort? Am I expecting the individual to do something which is too difficult? Will the individual have the determination to change and then sustain that change? Above all, in the counseling interview, the need to change has to be presented in such a way as to secure the willingness to change.

The formula has interesting relevance to career discussions. The individual may aspire to a larger position. He or she must be able to do the job. The individual must be better able than others to win out in the competition. Willingness has several facets. The individual must want the higher position. The individual must want it sufficiently to "pay what it costs," to make the investment needed to qualify and to perform the desired position.

Finally, we come to the removal interview. In making the decision to remove an individual from a position you have to work through the basic question of ability to perform satisfactorily and, possibly, the willingness to do so. A decidedly negative conclusion on either ability or willingness leads to the removal interview.

REQUIREMENTS FOR GETTING A CHANGE IN HABITS

Old dogs never learn! This cliche may be correct. Notice it doesn't say old dogs can't learn. One of the main reasons old dogs and young dogs do not learn is because they do not see any need to change. This also applies to old employees and young employees.

The performance and counseling interviews quite often identify a condition which requires that a subordinate change, that he or she give up a habit and develop a new one. Habits can be changed. Sometimes the process is discouragingly slow. Nevertheless, the manager and supervisor must persist.

Four conditions greatly facilitate getting a change in habits. The individual whose performance is to be changed must:

1. See and feel a need to change, to adopt a new way of behaving.
2. Develop skill and confidence in using a new habit.
3. Try out the new way.
4. Find out that the new way works, that it produces results desired (success).

Consideration of each of these points follows.

Need to Change

We noted early that individuals have a self-concept. This concept has been "hammered out" over a period of time. It derives from early childhood experiences and subsequent successes and failures. By the time an individual has reached the executive ranks, one's self-concept is quite firm. One might even say rigid. A need to change, therefore, runs full tilt into a stationary concept. As often as not, the "need to change" gets bruised.

The performance interview permits the superior to stress the variance between results and expectations and the need to remove the variance. Making the process a shared effort helps get the subordinate to see the need to change. In the counseling interview the problem of a change in habit gets tough. An individual is engaged in a behavior which is generally recognized as inappropriate. The individual is not likely to recognize the seriousness of the situation. Persistence in an inappropriate behavior is likely to have deep seated reinforcements. This becomes the first order of business in the counseling interview. In fact, several interviews may be needed to get the need to change seen and felt by the subordinate. In effect, you have to get the "willingness" portion of the previously discussed formula in operation.

Skill and Confidence

We can now shift from willingness to ability. The ability to change requires that an individual develop skill and confidence in using a new habit. A series of small, paced steps is far better than trying for one big step. It helps to be precise about the new habit. If skill is needed, then instruction or tutoring helps. Encouragement is critical in developing confidence. A "plan of action" step will be included in the performance interview, the counseling interview, and the career discussion. This step encourages the application of the above suggestions.

The New Habit

Have you ever tried to break an egg cautiously? Sometimes individuals have this same hesitancy when it comes to changing managerial habits. The effort is too slow, too cautious, too timid. The individual must be encouraged to try the new alternative. In some instances more than encouragement is required. A strong "push" may be needed.

Success

Hopefully, the application of the changed habit results in success. The individual then becomes eligible for one or more of the factors previously discussed about feeling successful. One's self-concept is enhanced. Pride takes over. A sense of achievement occurs. You are now likely to see a habit change. Occasionally, you are disappointed. At least you can salvage your own concept as a "teacher." You have done your best. I once met a pro golf instructor who taught by a certain method. He held himself to high standards on the application of his method. This overcame his frustration when his pupils made little or no progress. You might find yourself doing the same with some "difficult-to-change" individuals.

THE USE OF BOTH POSITIVE AND NEGATIVE MOTIVATION

It isn't quite accurate to say a manager motivates a subordinate. Motivation is a condition, within an individual, which stimulates the individual to act, to behave, to perform, to do.

An individual is said to be positively motivated when he or she acts so as to gain something that is desired. The gain may be praise, promotion, or some other type of reward. It may be a sense of achievement or winning in competition.

An individual is said to be negatively motivated when he or she acts so as to avoid something considered undesirable. The individual may desire to avoid criticism, to avoid being punished or removed from a position.

An executive has a variety of rewards and penalties available to use for motivational purposes. We have asked thousands of managers to report on the way their superior uses both praise and criticism. Amazingly, half of the managers report that their superior doesn't use either. It is true, however, that criticism is likely to occur more often than praise.

The current stress on human relations has led some executives to assume that one doesn't use negative motivation. In our experience, an effective executive will likely use both. However, the positive approach will be exhausted before turning to the negative type. There are good reasons for doing this. It goes back to the definition of motivation as an internal condition. Our objective is to have an individual who is *self-motivated,* one who is high in willingness. He or she goes ahead whether the superior is there or not.

Here is where negative motivation has its limitations:

It Is Unpredictable

Sometimes a heavy use of fear will get unexpected results. For example, some executives demand an improvement in reported results. Under severe pressure some subordinates may report in such a way as to avoid criticism. This vicious circle leads to an unpleasant surprise for the superior which leads to more negative motivation. One executive moved into a new organization. He called all the managers together and informed them they were incompetent. Immediately thereafter, the group went "all out" to prove him wrong. Subsequently, the same executive moved to a new organization and gave the same speech. This time the group agreed with him. There was no response. The former group still had pride and resilience. The latter group did not.

It Is Not Sustaining

The executive, in effect, has to "prime the pump" each time; there isn't a continuous flow. An executive might be able to run a small organization and provide all the stimulus. However, few can do it for a large organization. The burden of building up willingness and sustaining it becomes extremely difficult if one relies heavily on negative motivation.

It Often Inhibits Action

Individuals begin to limit their responses, to restrict the risks they take, to play it safe. Their role is one of a "low profile."

In some organizations subordinates will admit they follow a "low-profile" role. It is interesting to watch some executives using negative motivation in hopes of getting more entrepreneurial behavior. Subordinates persist in pushing problems up to the executives for solution. One executive of this type complained that his subordinates had an uncanny ability to delegate upward.

It May Lead to Conformity

Individuals may, for example, do exactly as they are told, even when they know it is wrong. The extreme occurs when subordinates rush out to do what they know to be wrong and do it enthusiastically.

ENVIRONMENTAL OR CLIMATE FACTORS

Over a period of years we have sent a survey, entitled a Climate Survey, to thousands of managers. The task requires that survey participants report how important they consider each factor. The participants also indicate their present level of satisfaction.

An example of a survey questionnaire follows:

Climate Survey

Instructions:

Twenty-six factors are of concern to managers like yourself have been listed in this Climate Survey. Two questions are asked about each factor. In the left-hand column check how important each factor is to you *personally*. In the right-hand column check how *personally* satisfied you are with the factor.

(Participants are then given an opportunity to give written comments to fully express themselves. We will not report on the written comments.)

1. Having a position in which the work itself is interesting and enjoyable?

   How interesting and enjoyable your work is:

a. Of great importance.	*a.* I am well satisfied.
b. Of considerable importance.	*b.* I am satisfied.
c. Somewhat importance.	*c.* I am not satisfied.
d. Not important.	*d.* I am quite dissatisfied.
e. Does not apply.	*e.* Does not apply.

Table 1 shows the results for 26 factors. We will limit our attention to the data pertaining to importance.

It is interesting to note that all factors are considered important by three fourths or more of the survey participants. It isn't until one looks at the factors that are considered "very important" that you get a real wide spread in the results. It is apparent, for example, that compensation is much lower in importance than having interesting and enjoyable work.

We have not referred to Herzberg's[2] two-factor theory of motivation for a very specific reason. We think the dichotomy developed by Herzberg between so-called motivators and

TABLE 1

Importance of Climate Survey Factors*

		Percent Saying Either "Very Important" or "Important"	Percent Saying "Very Important"
1.	Interesting and enjoyable work..	100	72
2.	Knowing your organization's goals and objectives..........................	100	71
3.	Having a position which makes full use of your abilities......................	100	69
4.	Having a capable manager..................	99	56
5.	Having a good idea of what is expected of you in your job.................	98	68
6.	Promotions go to those best qualified.....................................	97	66
7.	Knowing what your manager thinks about your performance.....................	97	47
8.	Manager who is concerned about development of personnel....................	97	41
9.	Being part of a component that has influence on critical decisions...........	96	54
10.	Manager receptive to new ideas.............	96	49
11.	Being treated fairly..........................	94	57
12.	Having advancement opportunities......................................	94	56
13.	Receiving information about what is going on in the organization.................................	94	41
14.	Working for an organization of which you can be proud...................	93	56
15.	Sense of direction in organization...........	93	52
16.	Freedom to run own job......................	91	51
17.	Manager who sets high standards...........	91	51
18.	Compensation.............................	88	50
19.	Career progress discussions.................	88	37
20.	Working for a company of which you can be proud...........................	87	49
21.	Receiving recognition for work you have accomplished.....................	86	45
22.	Sense of urgency in organization............	80	23
23.	Effective working relationship, own-other groups..........................	78	34
24.	Steady employment.........................	78	34
25.	Clear lines of authority......................	77	31
26.	Effective working relationships with other similar groups...................	73	43

*A full explanation of the Climate Survey is given in the author's book, entitled *Diagnostic Studies.*[1] (See Bibliography for details on numbered references.) The above table is based upon results from more than 3,000 managers, technical, and professional employees in 30 quite diverse organizations. The results are likely to be representative of business and manufacturing organizations in the United States.

hygienic factors is an artifact of the way Herzberg asked his basic research questions. The two-factor theory has stimulated much additional research and considerable controversy among psychologists. However, we prefer not to limit our consideration of environmental or climate factors. We have found situations where additions to the above list of 26 factors had to be made because of unique circumstances.

It is interesting to look at an a priori cluster of factors for the 18 highest ranked factors (using "very important" as the measure). Not all factors will be utilized.

As we look at the cluster of factors it is apparent that the position is a most important element for all managers. This confirms our earlier discussion of the importance of positions for individuals. The data on positions suggests that avoiding the Peter Principle, of putting an individual in a position where performance isn't satisfactory, is of great consequence to superior, subordinate, and the organization as a whole.

The Climate Survey also confirms McGregor's thesis that knowledge is vital to a subordinate's security. Two of the four items on knowledge are among the top ten in importance.

The importance of consistent discipline was stressed by McGregor. That premise is supported by the importance attached to the reward system.

It is interesting to note that factors pertaining to the position, knowledge required, and reward system are rated higher than superior and the larger organization. This confirms the phenomena of validation of one's self in a position. Individuals do prize independence as McGregor suggests.

A final comment. One is struck by the fact that 20 of the factors were considered as important or very important by 90 percent of the managers completing the survey.

There has been a tendency to try to reduce motivation to simple two-dimensional explanations. Herzberg contends factors are either "motivating" or "hygienic." While the

	Rank in Importance
Factors related to a *position*:	
Interesting and enjoyable work..........................	1
Having a position which makes full use of your abilities...	3
Having freedom to perform.............................	12
Factors relating to *knowledge:*	
Knowing one's organization's goals and objectives........	2
Having good idea of what is expected of you in your job......................................	4
Knowing what your manager thinks of your performance...	17
Receiving information about what is going on in the organization....................................	21
Factors relating to *superior:*	
Having a capable manager..............................	7
Having a manager who sets high standards..............	13
Having a manager who is receptive to new ideas..........	15
Having a manager who is concerned about development of personnel..............................	20
Factors relating to *reward system*	
Promotions going to those best qualified..................	5
Receiving recognition for work accomplished.............	18
Being treated fairly.......................................	6
Having advancement opportunities......................	8
Working where poor performers aren't rewarded the same as good performers................	26
Compensation..	14
Factors relating to the *larger organization*:	
Being part of an organization that has influence on critical decisions.........................	10
Working for a subdivision of an organization of which you can be proud......................................	9
Working for a company of which you can be proud...	16
Sense of direction in organization........................	11

priority of the above categories support the items within Herzberg's two factors, we see little value in restricting oneself to two dimensions. It may be appropriate in considering ability and willingness to look at all the factors previously presented.

THE PYGMALION EFFECT

Sterling Livingston,[3] a professor of business administration at the Harvard Business School, found interesting parallelisms between George Bernard Shaw's *Pygmalion* and the impact of executives on their subordinates. Livingston argues that:

> Some managers always treat their subordinates in a way that leads to superior performance. But most managers, like Professor Higgins, unintentionally treat their subordinates in a way that leads to lower performance than they are capable of achieving. The way managers treat their subordinates is subtly influenced by what they expect of them. If a manager's expectations are high, productivity is likely to be excellent. If his expectations are low, productivity is likely to be poor. It is as though there were a law that caused a subordinate's performance to rise or fall to meet his manager's expectations.
>
> The powerful influence of one person's expectations on another's behavior has long been recognized by physicians and behavioral scientists and, more recently, by teachers. But heretofore the importance of managerial expectations for individual and group performance has not been widely understood.

Livingston contends that the evidence supports four rather provocative statements:

1. What a manager expects of his subordinates and the way he treats them largely determine their performance and career progress.
2. A unique characteristic of superior management is their ability to create high performance expectations that subordinates fulfill.
3. Less effective managers fail to develop similar expectations and, as a consequence, the productivity of their subordinates suffers.

4. Subordinates, more often than not, appear to do what they believe they are expected to do.

The importance of one's self-concept was well illustrated by one case study reported upon by Livingston. In an insurance organization one group, based upon past records, was identified as an "average" group. However, the manager of this group refused to believe that he was less capable than the manager of the so-called "super staff," or that his agents were less capable than the agents in the top group. Acting upon his own assumptions, he led his group to make a greater proportinate increase in productivity than the top group.

Livingston reports that:

> It is of special interest that the self-image of the manager of the "average" unit did not permit him to accept others' treatment of him as an "average" manager, just as Eliza Doolittle's image of herself as a lady did not permit her to accept others' treatment of her as a flower girl. The assistant manager transmitted his own strong feelings of efficacy to his agents, created mutual expectancy of high performance, and greatly stimulated productivity.

He goes on to explain that:

> Unsuccessful salesmen have great difficulty maintaining their self-image and self-esteem. In response to low managerial expectations, they typically attempt to prevent additional damage to their egos by avoiding situations that might lead to greater failure. They either reduce the number of sales calls they make or avoid trying to "close" sales when that might result in further painful rejection, or both. Low expectations and damaged egos lead them to behave in a manner that increases the probability of failure, thereby fulfilling their managers' expectations.

Early we highlighted McGregor's thesis that an atmosphere of approval was vital to an effective superior/subordinate relationship. Livingston lends support to McGregor with the following observation:

> Managers cannot avoid the depressing cycle of events that flow from low expectations merely by hiding their feelings from subordinates. If a manager believes a subordinate will perform poorly, it is virtually impossible for him to mask his expectations, because the message usually is communicated unintentionally, without conscious action on his part.
>
> Indeed, a manager often communicates most when he believes he is communicating least. For instance, when he says nothing, when he becomes "cold" and "uncommunicative," it usually is a sign that he is displeased by a subordinate or believes he is "hopeless." The silent treatment communicates negative feelings even more effectively, at times, than a tongue-lashing does. What seems to be critical in the communication of expectations is not what the boss says, so much as the way *he behaves.* Indifferent and noncommital treatment, more often than not, is the kind of treatment that communicates low expectations and leads to poor performance.

We discussed the following formula in an earlier chapter:

$$\text{Ability} \times \text{Willingness} = \text{Performance}$$

It is interesting to consider that the superior's expectation may have a powerful impact on the formula, particularly on the willingness factor.

It appears that managers are more effective in communicating low expectations to their subordinates than in communicating high expectations. It is astonishingly difficult, according to Livingston, for managers to recognize the clarity with which they transmit negative feelings to subordinates. Livingston observes that something takes place in the minds of superior managers that does not occur in the minds of those who are less effective. The answer, it appears, seems to be the superior's own self-concept. His or her own record of success gives the superior confidence in his or her own ability to select, train, and motivate subordinates.

Livingston concludes his provocative article with the following statement:

> Industry has not developed effective first-line managers fast enough to meet its needs. As a consequence, many companies are under-developing their most valuable resource—talented young men and women. They are incurring heavy attrition costs and contributing to the negative attitudes young people often have about careers in business.
>
> For top executives in industry who are concerned with the productivity of their organizations and the careers of young employees, the challenge is clear: it is to speed the development of managers who will treat their subordinates in ways that lead to high performance and career satisfaction. The manager not only shapes the expectations and productivity of his subordinates, but also influences their attitudes toward their jobs and themselves. If he is unskilled, he leaves scars on the careers of the young men, cuts deeply into their self-esteem, and distorts their image of themselves as human beings. But if he is skillful and has high expectations of his subordinates, their self-confidence will grow, their capabilities will develop, and their productivity will be high. More often than he realizes, *the manager is Pygmalion.*

INDIVIDUALS VISUALIZED AS ENERGY PACKAGES

Energy is a prime concern of all of us in this day of oil shortages, of conflicts over nuclear energy, and concern about lack of energy needed to accomplish the many purposes only energy can do. For this reason, it is provocative and helpful, though not entirely accurate, to consider each subordinate as an energy package. The package is made up of mental, physical, and emotional energy. The interesting question is what percentage of the available energy is applied to accomplishing the objectives of the enterprise? One can also ask what percentage is applied to achieving of an individual's own purposes?

Consider your subordinates for a moment. You likely have one who is a topflight performer, possibly an outstanding performer. At the other extreme is someone whose performance is just satisfactory, or possibly not satisfactory. The other subordinates fit in between these two extremes. What would it be like if all subordinates were to move up in performance even with your top performer? You would be pleased. They would be pleased. The organization would be pleased. It is an idealistic question but, nevertheless, states a long-term objective for every executive. It raises the issue, how can you get each "energy package" contributing at its optimum level?

The five interviewing skills stressed in this book are aimed directly at your continuum of talent. The basic question is can you apply the interviewing skills so you can secure a definite shift toward the "outstanding" end of the continuum?

The selection interview should increase the likelihood that all additions will be quite satisfactory performers. The performance interview should help you get substantial improvement in current performance. The counseling interview should help to eliminate or reduce distracting or disqualifying behavior. Career discussions should assist in relating personal career goals with organizational needs and realities. The removal interview is a drastic step that removes individuals who are on the low end of the continuum.

In summary, the five interviews are not an end in themselves. They are a means to an end—optimum application of energy for the benefit of the subordinate as well as you and your organization.

part two

The Selection Challenge

IN RECENT YEARS presidents of a large oil company, of a large bank, and of a large airline, were replaced within about one year of their appointment. As these changes were announced in the business press it was apparent to everyone that serious mistakes had been made in their initial appointment. It is impossible to estimate the cost of such mistakes. Certainly, it was costly to executive morale. It also was likely that competitive position on sales and profits was lost. These three initial decisions and the subsequent reversal represents both the importance and the difficulty of the selection challenge.

There are several reasons why the selection challenge is difficult. One reason is that the selection decisions at the executive level are few and far between. This means that the opportunity to apply one's skill occurs infrequently hence little improvement occurs. A second reason is that few executives have mastered the fundamentals of selection, they haven't mastered a process. A third reason is that few large organizations have a systems approach to executive continuity. A fourth reason is that the selection challenge is much more difficult than it appears.

Observation of a large number of executives over a period

of years leads me to conclude that very few executives improve in their ability to handle the selection challenge. Part II is devoted to overcoming this pattern. Chapter 4 deals with the selection process. A five-step process will be recommended. Chapter 5 will be devoted to the selection interview. The selection interview is designed for the executive to use when a candidate is not well known. Chapter 6 considers the selection decision. This decision involves matching candidates against specifications.

4

The Selection Process

As NOTED EARLIER, few executives improve upon their "batting average" in making appointments to executive positions. One reason is the lack of a process. A process involves being systematic about the major steps involved in making a selection decision. A five-step process will be recommended. Let us first consider the five steps. Then attention will be given to each step in turn. The five steps are:

Step 1: Define specifications required to achieve desired objectives.
Step 2: Identify several worthy candidates.
Step 3: Interview worthy candidates.
Step 4: Secure additional data.
Step 5: Make decision on candidates versus specifications.

STEP 1: DEFINE SPECIFICATIONS REQUIRED TO ACHIEVE THE DESIRED OBJECTIVES

Specifications define those characteristics of an individual which are considered necessary if the individual is to perform satisfactorily upon being appointed to a position. Many an executive skips this initial step. Actually, this isn't quite accurate. One can't avoid making some assumptions about what is required. The real issue is one of thoroughness. In addition to being thorough, it is vital that one's choice of specifications be accurate. Attention will be given to various types of specifications. The variation in types will permit a decision upon the thoroughness or complexity with which you wish to prepare specifications.

Suggestions on the preparation of specifications will be made. These suggestions should help with the challenge of identifying those specifications which are most critical to successful performance. Once prepared, the specifications need to be used and used effectively. Numerous uses of specifications will be described.

Some readers are already using a thorough process with regard to specifications. In that case, you can contrast your current approach with the one recommended here. Hopefully, some "polishing" and "perfecting" of your process will result.

Types of Specifications

Some organizations prepare a job or position specifications along with a job or position description. They are often referred to as a "generic" specifications. In effect, the specifications are general ones, considered relevant for a given position for the foreseeable future.

The alternative to a "generic" specifications is one prepared when a given position is open. The specifications pertain to a particular position at a given point in time. Step 1, by implication, implies that the alternative to a generic specifications is to be preferred. This is true. A specification will be much more helpful if it is prepared for a specific position which is to be filled shortly.

A second way of differentiation among specifications has to do with their length or comprehensiveness. We will use three types, defined as follows:

1. Short type (make or break).
2. Intermediate type.
3. Comprehensive type.

Let us consider several examples of each type.

Short Types of Specifications

Position Specifications for
Plant Manager of Plant X

1. Must be experienced with unionizing campaigns.

2. Must be knowledgable of new manufacturing processes.

3. Must be willing to live in a small city.

4. Must be willing to stay in this position for four to six years.

5. Demonstrated ability to get good operating results from medium-sized plant.

Position Specifications for
Product General Manager
in Location A

1. Tough-minded and demanding; capable of turning around an unsatisfactory business.

2. Skillful in negotiating with customers, suppliers, and unions.

3. Considerable experience with given product line (because this is a long-cycle business).

4. Demonstrated ability to select competent people and develop managerial depth.

5. Capable of moving on to a bigger position within three to five years.

6. Experienced doing business offshore (particularly Europe).

Intermediate Types of Specifications

Position Specifications for
a Group Vice President
for Group X

1. Demonstrated ability to manage a successful business at the division level.

2. Definitely entrepreneurial, growth oriented.

3. Skillful in business planning (long and short term).

4. Able to command the respect of experienced division general managers (some of whom think they should have been appointed).

5. Effective in interacting and influencing high-level individuals in corporation, in regulatory agencies, and in customer organizations.

6. Good grasp of technical aspects of businesses in the group.

7. Knowledgable about global aspects of doing business in product lines in group.

8. Knowledgable about the corporation, in policies and ways of doing things.

9. Willing to work in a metropolitan city.

10. Understands the intricacies of matrix organization (a matrix structure reports to group level).

Position Specifications for
a Chief Engineer of a
Large Central Engineering Department

1. A solid knowledge of the technology. Shrewd in anticipating trends.

Intermediate Types of Specifications (*continued*)

2. Considerable experience in directing smaller engineering departments.

3. High standards in all areas. Demanding of self and others.

4. Astute in making trade-off decisions to get optimum engineering results for the investment.

5. Demonstrated ability to select competent people and replace nonperformers.

6. Effective in interacting with operating divisions. Commands respect of other executives.

7. Skillful in negotiating with and getting results from outside contractors.

8. Demonstrated ability to manage prima donnas, to get teamwork.

9. Integrity of highest order.

10. Skillful in managing project-type organization.

11. Concerned about and skillful in personnel administration.

12. Knowledgable about global aspects of engineering projects.

13. High in initiative. A self-starter.

14. Experience in several of the operating groups.

15. Skillful in communicating.

Comprehensive Type of Specifications

Store Manager
Large Retail Store

1. *Experience required*
   1.1. Total pertinent experience: Twelve to fifteen years minimum.
   1.2. Merchandising experience:
       a. Five years merchandise manager, preferably in more than one division.
       b. Three years department manager.
   1.3. Staff function: Two years desirable.
   1.4. Demonstrated profit-making ability and increase sales.

2. *Specialized knowledge*
   2.1. Areas requiring complete familiarity:
       a. Buying.
       b. Selling:
           (1) Customer relations.
           (2) Organizing for selling.
       c. Sales promotion:
           (1) Merchandise presentation.
           (2) Planning sales attack.
       d. Stock management:
           (1) Assortment development.
           (2) Investment.
           (3) Turnover.
   2.2. Areas requiring general familiarity:
       a. Control:
           (1) Financial.
           (2) Systems.
       b. Operations.
       c. Personnel.
       d. Sales promotion—technical aspects of advertising and display.

Comprehensive Type of Specifications (*continued*)

3. *Education and/or advanced training required*
    Bachelor's degree. Company executive training program, external management training (AMA, NRMA, etc.) to update knowledge of general manager; personal development program.

4. *Managerial ability*
    4.1. Planning: Demonstrated ability to do both long- and short-range planning. Ability to coordinate planning in all major functions to maximize store sales and profits. Converts commitments into tasks and allocates resources to fulfill these commitments.
    4.2. Organizing: Demonstrated understanding of organization principles and theory. Ability to set up and maintain a simple, flexible organization.
    4.3. Leadership: Demonstrated ability to lead, inspire, gain respect, and get maximum output from subordinates.
    4.4. Controlling: Demonstrated ability to operate within all established budgets and policies, financial and otherwise.
    4.5. Selecting and developing personnel: Ability to develop an effective and productive executive organization and to eliminate incompetents.

5. *Personal characteristics*
    5.1. Aggressiveness: demonstrated ability to produce results. High personal energy level and aggressiveness.
    5.2. Integrity: Consistent in actions, ability to make tough decisions, stands on principles, open-minded, and frank.
    5.3. Judgment: Demonstrated ability to make sound, difficult decisions. Ability to decide priorities and keep eye on them.

Comprehensive Type of Specifications (*continued*)

5.4. Emotional stability: Ability to operate under pressure; not easily frustrated; self-control.

5.5 Expression: Must have ability to communicate with others. Ability to sell oneself, one's ideas, and one's organization to customers, staff, management, and the business community. Must have ability to write clearly and concisely.

5.6. Risk taking: Demonstrated willingness to take risks. Makes good decisions more often than not in the absence of all known facts.

5.7. Creativity: Ability to see and adopt new methods to fit the changing needs of store.

5.8. Ambition: Strong personal drive to succeed and to assume greater responsibility.

6. *Relationships*

6.1. Ability to establish and maintain effective working relationships.

7. *Physical characteristics*

7.1. Health: Good physical condition; no known limitations; personal vitality.

7.2. Appearance: Presentable and should possess outgoing personality.

Top Functional Manager Specifications
Systems Engineering

1. *Experience required*

1.1. Total amount of pertinent experience: Ten years minimum experience, 15 years desirable.

1.2. Total amount of managerial experience: Two to three assignments at subsection level.

Comprehensive Type of Specifications (*continued*)

2. *Specialized knowledge*
   2.1. Areas requring complete familiarity:
       a. Systems engineering:
           (1) Synthesis to satisfy customer requirements.
           (2) Reduce requirements to specifications (in conjunction with equipment designers).
       b. Hardware Engineering:
           (1) Prime electronics/electromechanical technologies.
           (2) Design.
       c. Field operations:
           (1) Types of work needed to support product in field.
           (2) Technical support.
           (3) Installation.
           (4) Testing.
           (5) Coping with geographic dispersion.
   2.2. Areas requiring general familiarity:
       a. Production/manufacturing: Through design exposure process.
       b. Customer:
           (1) How products fit customer mission/needs.
           (2) How customer does business.
       c. Internal business system:
           (1) How work flows through the shop.
           (2) Engineering part in overall business.

3. *Education and/or advanced training required*
   Four-year college degree. Company training program and/or masters degree desirable. Continual updating of individual's functional discipline.

Comprehensive Type of Specifications (*continued*)

4. *Managerial ability*
   4.1. Planning: Demonstrated ability to do both long- and short-range planning. Evidence that long-range plans were established and accomplished. Demonstrated ability to: establish expense and investment budgets; establish manpower requirements; schedule work; convert commitments into tasks and allocate resources to fulfill these commitments.
   4.2. Organizing: Demonstrated understanding of organization principles and theory. Matches men with jobs. Keeps flexibility in organization. Structures work to meet objectives.
   4.3. Motivation: Demonstrated ability to lead, inspire, and gain respect of subordinates.
   4.4. Controlling: Demonstrated ability to operate within budget and established schedules. Knows what is going on in his or her component.
   4.5. Selecting and developing personnel: Demonstrated ability to select competent people and to replace incompetents. Also must have ability to develop subordinates as demonstrated by the number of employees promoted from his or her organization, replacement strengths, approach to personnel development (etc.).

5. *Personal characteristics*
   5.1. Drive: Demonstrated ability to produce results. High personal energy level.
   5.2. Integrity: Says what he or she believes, admits mistakes, tough decisions based on principle. No evidence should exist of any lack of integrity.
   5.3. Judgment: Demonstrated ability to make sound, difficult decisions. Considers total business in making decisions.
   5.4. Emotional stability: Ability to handle a number of different assignments under pressure. Not easily frustrated. Ability to control temper.

Comprehensive Type of Specifications (*concluded*)

    5.5. Expression: Must have ability to communicate effec-
tively with others, particularly the ability to sell
oneself, one's ideas, and one's organizations to customers, external and internal. Must have ability to
write clearly and concisely.

    5.6. Risk taking: Demonstrated willingness to do the
novel and the new. Makes good decision more often
than not in the absence of all known facts.

    5.7. Technical Competence: Ability to understand techni-
cal aspects of function and project an image of technical competence. Ability to quickly understand a
problem, analyze the alternatives and to make sound
decisions.

6. *Physical characteristics*

    6.1. Health: Good physical condition—no known limita-
tions.

    6.2. Appearance: Neat personal appearance.

Preparation of Specifications

Let's assume you have decided upon one of the three types
of specifications just discussed. Now comes the tough part.
What specifications are really essential? Here is where
shrewd judgment is required. Let us consider nine ways to
prepare specifications in an effective manner.

1. Don't Leave It Up to the Staff. There is a tendency
for a line or operating manager to think that specifications
preparation is something which can be delegated. It can be,
but not without risk. The risk is that the selection decision is
handicapped from the very beginning by inappropriate specifications. Deciding on the right specifications is a skill. Prac-
ticing that skill, whenever possible, is desirable. In truth, the

preparation of specifications requires a modest amount of time. If you are inclined to delegate this step, you might very well question your entire attitude toward the selection process.

2. Do Use Multiple Inputs.   In most organizations a given executive decides on an appointment, but it must be approved by a higher level executive. It is helpful to have the higher level executive prepare a set of his or her own specifications. If this can't be done, then let the higher level executive review and modify the specifications prepared by the appointing executive.

3. Look at Business or Operating Objectives.   You are selecting an individual who will be expected to accomplish rather specific business or operating objectives. It is extremely helpful in identifying specifications to review business or operating objectives. They should pertain to the next year or possibly next three years. The more urgent objectives, the more difficult objectives practically force you to consider specifications which will be needed if they are to be achieved.

If a business is "sick" and a major turn around is desired, it is obvious that an experienced executive is needed who can size up the situation both accurately and quickly. In addition, the executive must be demanding, willing to make and implement adverse decisions.

Other specifications could be mentioned, but the above example illustrates the value of referring to business or operating objectives.

4. Review the Position Description.   Most organizations are in the habit of preparing a position description. Let's assume the position description is up-to-date. It should contain a list of the important tasks, duties, and responsibilities of the position under consideration. Here again, a review of such a document does help to identify needed specifications.

A responsibility to review and approve major capital appropriation requests certainly leads to the conclusion that business acumen, technological know-how, and marketing "instincts" are needed specifications.

5. *Consider Present and Past Incumbents.* It is easy to think of specifications when one considers present or past incumbents. If the individual was a success, what personal factors came into play? If the individual did not succeed, again, what personal factors came into play? Of course, one has to be alert to future changes which will require different personal factors from those which operated in the past.

It is often beneficial to get several independent judgments of specifications suggested by analysis of incumbents.

There is one interesting phenomena to watch. It is called the "mirror image" phenomena. You, of course, consider yourself successful. Therefore, the specifications you select are those you see yourself possessing. Hence, the term "mirror image." The challenge here is to be accurate in one's introspections.

6. *Analyze Relevant Competitors.* It is an interesting exercise to identify an individual holding a comparable position in a competitor's organization. What are some personal factors that seem to be behind their advantages? Behind their disadvantages? Often individuals in your organization possess inputs relevant to these questions.

7. *Give Attention to Future Changes.* Often major trends are apparent in an industry which will require a different type of executive in the future. Similarly, an entire function, such as personnel or finance, may be changing radically. The executive in charge of these functions in the future may need to be drastically different from those in the past.

8. *Separate Critical from the "Nice to Have."* One can easily make a long list of desirable specifications. However, some are absolutely critical. They are "make or break" specifications. Their presence makes for success; their absence makes for failure. It is helpful to separate those specifications deemed to be an absolute must.

In my experience, the weighting of specifications doesn't really help much. However, it certainly does help to have the "must" specifications identified.

It is also necessary to relate the specifications to the salary level of the position. The salary level has to insure getting the "must" items. It is unlikely it will be high enough to insure getting all the "nice-to-have" items.

9. Don't Build in "Crutches" in Advance. In preparing specifications some specifications are discounted because the immediate supervisor feels he or she can fulfill a given need. In effect, you are building in a crutch in advance. This discounting often occurs as you get down to the final decision. For example, one individual met all of the must requirements; however, it was obvious this individual missed on "effective communications." The superior rationalized that the executive would either be tutored on this or that the necessary presentations would be made for the executive. It is desirable to avoid these built-in "crutches" if at all possible. They will still occur, let's just not build them in in advance.

Uses of Specifications

There are many uses which can be made of specifications. Let us consider some of the more frequent ones.

1. Initial Selection Process. The preparation of a specification helps in the initial selection process. It may suggest the necessity to look outside one's own organization.

It may suggest that getting a number of candidates will be easy or, maybe, just the reverse. It may suggest the need to bring in an outside recruiter. If one does this, the outside recruiter will certainly begin by consideration of specifications.

2. Final Selection Decision. Here is where specifications play a critical role. Several candidates are matched against the specifications. It is possible none qualify. Maybe several do. How to be objective? How to select the best qualified? Here is where a good set of specifications will come in handy.

3. Thinking through a Staffing Problem. Sometimes an incumbent isn't performing up to expectations. This is an anguishing period. Can a change on the superior's part make a difference? Sometimes it's like asking can the alcoholic be cured? A retroactive analysis of how well the incumbent meets the specifications for the position can help crystallize one's thinking.

4. Replacement Planning. Often an executive is required to identify individuals who can be a replacement. Possibly multiple evaluations are called for. The accuracy of replacement planning decisions can be enhanced considerably by referring to relevant specifications.

5. Career Discussions. Career discussions will be dealt with in Part Five. Specifications will prove to be a useful tool in—

a. Informing an individual of the specifications of a coveted position.
b. Assessing how well an individual meets specifications.
c. Informing the individual of the assessment.
d. Planning appropriate developmental actions to meet future specifications.

STEP 2: IDENTIFY SEVERAL WORTHY CANDIDATES

This step is a crucial one. One's batting average on selection decisions is closely related to the number of candidates, worthy ones, available for consideration.

A chief executive of a large enterprise set the following objective for their executive continuity effort. The executive continuity effort would be considered a success if they had three qualified internal candidates to choose from in making appointments to key positions. Interestingly, in spite of extensive and consistent efforts over a period of years, the best estimate is that two qualified candidates are now available.

Time does not permit describing the requirements for a systems approach to executive continuity.* Attention will be given to (1) the securing of candidates from one's own organization, (2) from internal sources outside your own organization, and (3) from external sources. The advantage of (4) a "scouting" process will also be discussed.

Securing of Candidates from One's Own Organization

In some instances replacement charts will have been prepared in advance. Referral to these charts will identify possible candidates. It is interesting to note that this step is often overlooked. Replacement charts are prepared to meet a deadline for submission "upstairs." They aren't referred to when the time comes to make an appointment. Studies conducted in a large number of organizations reveal that the candidate finally selected often doesn't appear on replacement charts.

---

* Thorough coverage of the challenge of executive continuity has been given in Mahler and Wrightnour, *Executive Continuity*, Dow Jones-Irwin, Homewood, Ill.

This just means that the mechanics of replacement are in place. The routine is carried out. However, the process is not generating sound, useful data. The process is not being used.

Time doesn't permit suggesting how to improve upon replacement planning. However, when replacement charts or tables are available we urge reference to them. This will provide pressure for subsequent upgrading the soundness of the process. Another alternative is to request nominations from appropriate individuals in your own organization. Some organizations are "posting" openings so that individuals can apply for consideration of available openings. Few individuals have a neutral position on posting. They are either for it or against it. Its value can best be tested in terms of the objectives of your own organization.

Internal Sources Outside Your Own Organization

Most organizations now have a central personnel group who maintain personnel records on all personnel. Consultation with this group will often generate candidates to be considered. Often the consultation is required as part of the standard operating procedure.

Many an executive makes use of the old, tried, and true alternative—that of calling a trusted friend and asking for nominations.

External Sources

When thorough review of internal talent reveals none who meet the specifications, it becomes necessary to "go outside." Two alternatives exist—advertising and use of executive recruiting. Both are worth considering. Advertising is obviously the more economical. The search through the pile of resumes to find the well qualified is certainly a task.

Recruiters can make a real contribution, particularly at higher levels. Some companies get their money's worth from a given recruiter. Other companies fail to. Those successful companies do their homework. They have well thought out specifications, they have a competitive compensation package put together, they interview candidates quickly and arrive at conclusions quickly.

Companies experienced in working with recruiters will quite likely turn down the first few candidates. You get past the "readily available" candidates in this manner. The "quick" candidates are often "also rans" in a recent assignment for some other company. You need to encourage the recruiter to "dig"—that is, to do an intensive search for presently employed candidates.

Scheduling interviews on short notice is helpful. However, the interviews need to be planned carefully. We describe an interview process in the next chapter you will find helpful. We suggest you complete your selection interview first. If the decision is likely to be negative, you invest a limited time after the selection interview.

If the individual appears to be a possible choice, then you invest time in informing him or her about your organization. We see little value in either party playing games at this stage. The positives and negatives of a position need to be looked at closely to avoid the following situation.

One executive was recently selected for a key position. He lives in a major city 400 miles from the new organization. After two weeks in the new position he called off moving. He isn't yet sure he will like the new company. Eighteen months have gone by; commuting is getting tougher. The issue begs for resolution.

The final decision requires critical evaluation of each candidate against the specifications.

Scouting System

Some top executives have decided to operate their own "scouting" system. They are on the lookout, at all times, for talented people. In all contacts in the industry and in other situations, the executive ferrets out names of individuals considered to be quite talented. A record system is maintained for future use. Often the executive makes it a point to get acquainted with the talented individuals. In some instances, subordinates are encouraged to do the same thing. It is amazing how diligence and a small amount of time spent in "scouting" does produce vitally needed talent.

STEP 3: INTERVIEW WORTHY CANDIDATES

Matching candidates against the specifications (requires that you have considerable knowledge of each candidate.) In some instances, a candidate has worked under your direct supervision so that you have firsthand knowledge. In other instances, you may only have casual knowledge of the candidate or you may not know the candidate at all. In these instances an interview is a must. Some executives, feeling uncomfortable about their skill, delegate the interview. In my opinion, the success of an executive hinges so directly on choice of subordinates that each executive must make the selection decision. It helps in making the decision to have done a thorough interview.

In this chapter attention will be given to the requirements for an effective interview. Suggestions for conducting an actual interview will be featured in the next chapter.

Requirements for an Effective Interview

1. The real challenge is to have a pleasant talk and yet secure sufficient data to arrive at a confident decision. So it is necessary to carry out a pleasant communication process and, at the same time, carry out an analytical, evaluative process.

2. The interview process is best conducted by using a well-selected set of questions. The specific questions I recommend will be given in the next chapter. The questions are designed to explore two major areas: accomplishments and management processes.

3. Journalistic questions are preferred. They get their name from journalists who rigorously search for descriptive facts, eschewing opinion and hearsay.

4. In addition to the basic questions, skillful use of "probe" questions adds to the value of the information to be secured in the interview.

5. In effect, the interviewer may be said to be taking a "Polaroid picture" of accomplishments. Questions are asked until a clear-cut picture is secured of just what was accomplished. Similarly, questions are asked until a clear-cut picture is obtained of the management processes used by the candidate.

6. The interviewer is responsible for controlling the use of interview time. The prepared questions help. However, the intent is to get as much descriptive information as possible in a limited length of time.

7. The interviewer needs to realize that the entire sequence involves developing hypotheses and testing them. Does the interviewee meet each specification or not? The interviewer usually starts, before the interview, with some preliminary hypotheses. During the interview the inter-

viewer endeavors to gain confidence in strong positive positions or strong negative positions. The positions are not based on feel or gut-reaction, they are based on descriptive information.

STEP 4: SECURE OTHER DATA

At the executive level there are several sources of additional data. One is reference checks, a second is psychological tests. Let's consider each one in turn.

Reference Checks

It is likely that you have been called for a reference check. Do you remember how you responded? You mentioned several positives, important ones. You commented on one or, at most, two negatives, likely unimportant ones. In summary, you gave minimal information. It will require special effort to secure useful data from references. Consideration also must be given to the individuals given as references.

It is important that you identify the immediate superior for the last several positions. In some instances, the superior once removed should also be identified. Occasionally, a personnel officer who is well acquainted with the candidate is worth including in the reference check.

A face-to-face interview is likely to secure greater cooperation and more complete information. The expense of such an interview has to be weighed against the importance of the appointment and the risk involved.

A telephone interview is a second way to get reference data. Your luck will vary. In some instances, you will get very useful data; in other instances, you won't. Nevertheless, the effort must be made.

It helps to use a regular set of interview questions. A set of such questions follows:

Reference Check Questions

1. How long did you supervise (name of candidate). _____

2. What were several of the candidate's more important accomplishments. (Use personal name rather than term "candidate.")

3. What would be one or two ways the candidate didn't come up to your expectations? I call them "disappointments."

4. Main reasons for the disappointments.

5. Where would you be inclined to give the candidate freedom and, where would you supervise the candidate more closely?

6. I'd be interested in the background on why the candidate is now available.

7. We are thinking of _____ for _____
   (candidate)   (mention title
   _____. What would you say are several of the
   of position)
   candidate's assets for such a position? What are two or three reservations you would have?

Experience suggests that a request of a reference for a written evaluation is likely to produce very little helpful information.

Psychological Tests

Psychological tests of executives have been in use for more than 30 years. Scores of psychologists devote full time to the process. Most are in consulting organizations. While tests have been around for a long time, they cannot be said to be widely used within organizations. A few organizations who are in the habit of using them are enthusiastic about them. Many organizations wouldn't consider using them under any circumstance.

Just what type of process constitutes a psychological evaluation and what data is provided. The evaluation process involves the use of several types of tests. Mental measurements are usually used. Interest inventories and personality characteristics are also used. An interview, usually referred to as a depth interview, is conducted.

The process produces a description of the personal characteristics of an individual. A primary virtue of a psychological evaluation is that the data is similar, so that comparisons can be made among several candidates.

A critical reservation is that the psychological evaluation provides little data pertaining to the specifications. Furthermore, big inferences have to be made from psychological characteristics to managerial abilities.

Our personal position is that psychological tests should not be used at the executive level. We do favor extensive use of tests for individuals early in their career.

STEP 5: MATCH CANDIDATES WITH SPECIFICATIONS

Now comes the critical point—the decision on whether a candidate meets the specifications. You have the following information:

1. Prior knowledge (if any).
2. Background data.
3. Interview of candidate on accomplishments.
4. Interview of candidate on managing processes.
5. Reference check inputs.

In some instances you may wish to have one or two other individuals interview the candidate. However, yours should be the thorough, decisive interview.

The more often a strength or weakness regarding a specification shows up in the above sources, the more confidence you can have in your interpretation.

You should be able to say:

Candidate meets the spec because . . . .

or

Candidate doesn't meet the specs as demonstrated by . . . .

5

The Selection Interview

THERE ARE TWO PARTS to the selection interview. Part one consists of getting the useful information. Part two is the interpretation and evaluation of the information. In Chapter 5 attention will be given to the challenge of getting useful information. Chapter 6 will be devoted to the interpretation of data.

THE INTERVIEW QUESTIONS

As mentioned in Chapter 4, a special set of journalistic type questions will be recommended. These questions have evolved over a period of years in a process we refer to as Accomplishment Analysis. The questions I recommend for use are listed below.

Selection Interview Questions

Preliminary:
1. Beginning with your move into your first supervisor job, would you tell me, briefly, *why each change was made.*

Accomplishments—Current Job:
2. Refer to most recent position. What would you say are some of your more important accomplishments? I'd be interested in operating results and any other accomplish-

ments you consider important. (Probe for four or five accomplishments. Get specific data.)

3. Considering these accomplishments, what are some of the reasons for your success?

4. Were there any unusual difficulties you had to overcome in getting these accomplishments?

5. What two or three things do you feel you have learned on this job?

6. What did you particularly like about the position?

7. There are always a few negatives about a position. What would you say you liked least about the position?

8. What responsibilities or results have not come up to your expectations? I'd be interested in things you had hoped and planned to accomplish which were not done. I sometimes call them disappointments. (Push for several, specific answers.)

9. What are some of the reasons for this?

Accomplishments—Second Position:

I'd like to talk with you about your experience as _____
_____. (Mention title of second most recent position.)

10. What would you say were some of the more important things you accomplished on this job?

11. What were some of the factors that would account for the accomplishments you have just mentioned?

12. What responsibilities or results didn't come up to your expectations on this job?

13. What were some of the reasons for this?

14. What would you say you learned on this job?

15. What did you like about it?

16. What didn't you like about it?

Selection Interview Questions *(continued)*

Additional Positions:

Repeat questions 10 through 16 if there was a significant period as a manager in a third position.

Planning, Decisions:

17. I'm interested in how you do your planning. What planning processes have you found useful and how do you go about them?

18. In what way do you feel you have improved in your planning in the last few years?

19. What are some examples of important types of decisions or recommendations you are called upon to make?

20. Would you describe how you went about making these types of decisions or recommendations. With whom did you talk, and so forth?

21. What decisions are easiest for you to make and which ones are more difficult?

22. Most of us can think of an important decision which we would make quite differently if we made it again. Any examples from your experience? Probe: What's the biggest mistake you can recall?

23. Most of us improve in our decision-making ability as we get greater experience. In what respects do you feel you have improved in your decision making?

Organization (Structure, Delegation, Staffing, Deselection, Transition):

24. What has been your experience with major expansion or reduction of force? (Explore for details.)

25. How many immediate subordinates have you selected in the last two years? How did you go about it? Any surprises or disappointments?

26. How many immediate subordinates have you removed from their jobs in the last few years? Any contemplated? One example of how you went about it.

27. How do you feel your subordinates would describe you as a delegator? Any deliberate tactics you use?

Controlling:

28. Some managers keep a very close check on their organization. Others use a loose rein. What pattern do you follow? How has it changed in the last few years?

29. What has been the most important surprise you have received from something getting out of control? Why did it happen?

30. Let's talk about standards of performance. How would you describe your own? What would your subordinates say? What would your boss say?

31. Sometimes it is necessary to issue an edict to an individual or the entire staff. Do you have any recent examples of edicts you have issued? Probe: Reasons? Results?

Supervision:

32. What things do you think contribute to your effectiveness as a supervisor?

33. From an opposite viewpoint, what do you think might interfere with your effectiveness as a supervisor?

34. In what respects do you feel you have improved most as a supervisor during the last few years?

35. What kind of supervisor gets the best performance out of you?

36. Some managers are quite deliberate about such things as communications, development, and motivation. Do you have any examples of how you do this?

37. What have you done about your own development in the last few years?

Selection Interview Questions (*concluded*)

Other:

38. Would you describe your relationship with your last three supervisors.

39. Considering your relationships both inside and outside the component, would you give me an example of where you have been particularly effective in relating with the others.

40. Would you also give me an example of where you might *not* have been particularly effective in relating with others.

41. Some people are short-fused and impatient in their reactions. How would you describe yourself?

42. Have you encountered any health problems? What do you do about your health?

43. Most of us can look back upon a new idea, a new project, or an innovation we feel proud of introducing. Would you describe one or two such innovations you are particularly proud of?

Future:

44. How do you feel about your progress (career-wise) to date?

45. What are your aspirations for the future? Have these changed?

46. We sometimes compare the assets and limitations of our products with competition. Let's do a related thing with your career. Thinking of your competition for jobs to which you aspire, what you say are your main assets, your strengths, and what would you say are your limitations? (Get three or more assets and three or more limitations.)

47. Are there any conditions of personal business, health, or family which would limit your flexibility for taking on a new assignment?

USE OF THE QUESTIONS

Answers should be obtained to all questions. Sometimes a given question is answered in response to an early question. Avoid asking a question if it has been answered earlier. We suggest you ask the questions the way they are worded. Use preambles to avoid a "third-degree" effect. The basic questions are "open-ended." You will need to use probes to get specific data. Probe to get an example, an illustration, a description of action taken. Endeavor, however, to keep a pleasant climate, one in which the interviewee is talking freely.

Remember: If you are to picture how an individual will perform in the future, you must have a clear, neat "mental picture" of how the individual has actually performed in the past.

SOME COMMON INTERVIEWING PITFALLS

1. Not asking questions clearly.
2. Interrupting when interviewee is doing his "preparatory thinking" before answering.
3. Cutting off responses interviewee thinks are important.
4. Overlooking "little clues" of a "big negative."
5. Probing beyond an interviewee's willingness to talk.
6. Permitting an interviewee to wander around.
7. Using leading questions. (Would you say . . . .?)
8. Asking questions which can be answered by a yes or no.

	Questions	
Specification Factors	*No.*	*Nature of Question*
Decision-making ability	20.	How decisions are made.
	21.	Easy and hard decisions.
	22.	Boner.
	23.	Improvement in decision-making.
Delegating ability	27.	Delegate as seen by subordinates.
Controlling ability	28.	Closeness of control.
	29.	Out-of-control situation.
	30.	Standards.
	31.	Edicts.
Development of personnel	36.	Deliberate actions.
	37.	Own development.
Organization planning	24.	Expansion and contraction.
Selection of personnel (deselection)	25.	Past experience with selection.
	26.	Nonperformers.
Planning ability	17.	Planning processes.
	18.	Improvement in planning.
Supervisory ability (leadership)	32.	Effectiveness.
	33.	Ineffectiveness.
	34.	Improvement made in supervisory ability.
	35.	Supervision preferred.
	36.	Specific practices.
Relationship	38.	Description of relationship with superiors.
	39.	Relationships inside and outside.
	40.	Ineffective examples.
	41.	Emotional reactions.
Innovativeness	43.	Examples of innovation.
Ambition	44.	Reaction to career progress.
	45.	States aspiration.
	47.	Limitations placed.

The second place to look for data about a given specification is the statement of accomplishments. In some instances there will be a direct relationship between a stated accomplishment and a given specification. In other instances, the reasons for accomplishment will provide interpretative clues.

The lack of accomplishments and reasons for this lack also contribute quite directly to interpretations regarding specifications.

The data on accomplishments may not contribute to every specification under consideration. Interpretation becomes challenging when there is conflict between accomplishment data and management process question results.

Another set of questions which provides data which assists in interpreting against specifications is the question of "likes" and "dislikes" for a given position.

In effect, the interpretation is a two-phase process. First, you are looking through several windows to get as accurate a picture as possible of what has happened in the past. Second, you look ahead and endeavor to visualize future performance.

Windows re Past
Performance

```
┌─────────────────────────┐
│                         │
│   Accomplishments       │
│   Position 1            │
│                         │
└─────────────────────────┘

┌─────────────────────────┐
│                         │
│   Accomplishments       │
│   Position 2            │
│                         │
└─────────────────────────┘

┌─────────────────────────┐
│                         │
│   Management            │
│   Processes             │
│                         │
└─────────────────────────┘
```

SUGGESTIONS REGARDING INDIVIDUAL SPECIFICATONS

The analogy to a Polaroid picture is pertinent here. Comprehensive inputs which form a consistent pattern give you a clean-cut focus on the past. In your interpretation you then use this focus on the past to decide how well specifications are met. Specifications are those things deemed essential for future success. We are relying heavily, therefore, on the past to make prediction about the future. This reliance may not be entirely justified at times, but it still provides the soundest basis we have available.

Let us take a specification, business judgment, and see how you go from interview data to interpretation against the specification.

There are many instances during an interview in which judgment shows up. The most important place is the inference one has to make as to the extent to which judgment accounts for accomplishments, and the extent to which poor judgment accounts for failure to accomplish results.

One gets some idea of judgment in terms of the responses of the interviewee. Does he or she readily grasp the question and respond in a direct manner? Does he or she have difficulty in grasping the question? Does he or she have difficulty in giving precise, coherent answers?

A major segment of the planning questions are devoted to this issue of judgment. Here one needs to look at the data for several questions such as the decisions permitted by one's superior, the decisions in which the boss has confidence and those where the boss does not. The interview questions do get descriptive data about the process by which the individual goes about arriving at decisions.

FINAL DECISION

The final interpretation is a "go" or "no-go" decision. The use of a Candidate Analysis Sheet will facilitate making the final decision. An example of such a sheet follows.

Candidate Analysis Sheet

Position Pooled Mngr.—Defense Analysis by: ___ *Date* ___

I. Results: List the five more important results he/she will
be expected to achieve.

1. Provide a sensitive and effective second avenue of
communications between customers and the top management of the group.

2. Develop sufficient stature to personally represent the
company at Washington conferences.

3. Upgrade the caliber of field personnel.

4. Direct effort aimed at identification of new business
opportunities for the group.

5. Secure and maintain confidence of division general
managers.

Candidate Analysis Sheet (*continued*)

		A	B	C	D	E
II.	**Requirements:** List the five more important requirements for success on the job.	III.	*Candidates versus Requirements:			
1.	Three or more years experience as a division general manager with a record of accomplishment.	1	1	3	2	5
2.	Personally compatible with president and division general managers.	2	1	3	3	4
3.	Skillful in communications, in influencing, in persuading, in establishing rapport with customers and influential men and women.	2	2	2	4	1
4.	Capable in administering a diverse group.	1	2	2	2	5
5.	Sound judgment on business, political, and technical problems (across spectrum of group business).	1	3	3	3	3
	Overall rating	1−	2+	3−	3+	5
	Ranking	1	2	3	4	5

* Rating:
1. Fully meets, no reservation.
2. Generally meets, minor reservation.
3. Generally meets, moderate reservation.
4. Generally meets, major reservation.
5. Fails to meet.

part three

The Performance Interview

DEFINITION

A PERFORMANCE INTERVIEW is a two-way dialogue between a superior and a subordinate about the latter's job performance. It is a review of accomplishments. It is a review of results. Often it has to do with a review of previously established objectives or goals.

THE NEED FOR PERFORMANCE INTERVIEWS

Over a period of years we have asked thousands of subordinates to report upon the coaching practices of their superiors. Some of the questions are quite pertinent to performance interviews. Let's consider the data for these questions.

Coaching Survey Results

		Percent
1.	In the last year has your superior talked with you about your evaluation of your performance of your major responsibilities?	
	a. No, this has not been done.	18
	b. My superior has done this in rather general terms...............................	32

Coaching Survey Results (*continued*)

		Percent

c. My superior has done this in some detail. . .   29

d. My superior has done this quite specifically.   21

Comment:

All the evidence points to the need to be quite specific, to get down to details when talking about performance. Otherwise change doesn't take place. The data suggests that half of the subordinates really get an effective or helpful performance appraisal. This is disturbing since most of the companies using the survey here long had a policy of formal annual performance appraisals.

2. How often in the last year has your superior discussed with you the results you have achieved on your financial responsibilities?

    a. My superior hasn't done this in the last year.   10

    b. My superior does this occasionally but in general terms.   35

    c. My superior does this occasionally but in rather specific terms.   40

    d. My superior does this frequently and in rather specific terms.   15

Comment:

Here again, the effective performance discussion would be one which gets down to specifics and does so either "occasionally" or "frequently." Almost one half of subordinates surveyed fail to get the benefit of such performance appraisals.

3. How often in the last year has your superior discussed with you the results you have achieved on your nonfinancial responsibilities?

    a. My superior hasn't done this in the last year.   10

Coaching Survey Results (*continued*)

---

b.	My superior does this occasionally but in general terms.	*Percent* 35
c.	My superior does this occasionally and in rather specific terms.	25
d.	My superior does this frequently and in rather specific terms.	25

Comment:

   Nonfinancial results are about the same as for financial results just reported. Again, half of the subordinates do not get the benefit of such performance interviews.

4. Has your superior had any discussions with you about ways in which you might improve your leadership or managing skills?

a.	My superior has not done this.	15
b.	My superior has done this in general terms.	35
c.	My superior has discussed one specific way.	25
d.	My superior has discussed two or more specific ways.	25

Comment:

   It is difficult to see how a superior can contribute to improving the managerial ability of subordinates if leadership and managing skills are not discussed in a specific manner. That same 50 percent are still neglected.

5. Have any group meetings been held in which your subordinates have reported to you and your superior on the progress they have made in achieving their objectives (goals, results)?

a.	This has never been done.	35
b.	This has been done once in the last two years.	10

Coaching Survey Results (*continued*)

---

c. This has been done about once in the last
two years. ....   *Percent*

    20

d. This has been done about two or more times
in the last year........................   35

Comment:

    Performance reviews can be done in a group
setting. It appears that about one half of the
subordinates have been involved in such a group
setting at least once or twice in the last few years.

6. To what extent do you and your superior agree
on the satisfactoriness of the results you have
achieved?

    a. I don't know if we agree or not.   15

    b. We agree as often as we disagree.   25

    c. We are in almost full agreement.........   50

    d. We are in full agreement.   10

Comment:

    A consequence of effective performance inter-
views would be an agreement on the part of both
parties about the satisfactoriness of the performance. The results are 60–40 on the positive
side. These results are consistent with results for
the first five questions noted above.

7. How well do you know what your superior thinks
of your performance (results, accomplishments) ?

    a. I don't know what my superior thinks of my
performance.   10

    b. I have some idea of what my superior thinks.   30

    c. I have a good idea of what my superior thinks.   45

    d. I have a very definite idea of what my supe-
rior thinks.   15

Coaching Survey Results (*concluded*)

Comment:	*Percent*
A frequently stated need is for subordinates to have knowledge of how their superior thinks of their performance. McGregor stressed this, as we noted in Chapter 1. About 60 percent have this need met.	

8. How helpful has your superior been in your development and growth over the last few years?

a.	My superior has helped very little.	15
b.	My superior has helped somewhat.	40
c.	My superior has helped considerably.	30
d.	My superior has helped a great deal.	15

Comment:
   One would expect subordinates to consider a superior who does effective performance interviews as one who has helped them develop and grow. Amazingly, less than half say the help has been "considerable" or "a great deal."

Overall Comment:
   It is generally agreed that performance appraisals should be done and done effectively. Half of the executives surveyed are reported as doing performance appraisals. Half are reported as providing knowledge of results.

The result of the above survey says that attention needs to be given to both developing a skill and overcoming the rather strong and persistent resistance of superiors to performance interviews. Guidelines will be suggested, followed by discussion of four types of performance interviews. The guidelines should help with the skill issue. Each executive will have to face up to his or her own attitude toward the performance interview process.

Performance interviews can be considered successful when—

1. Both parties discuss their own evaluations in a forth-right manner.
2. Differences are resolved. Negative variances are identi-fied.
3. Causes for negative variances are explored thoroughly.
4. Appropriate action plans are prepared.
5. Subsequently, satisfactory performance is secured.

One might diagram the performance interview as follows:

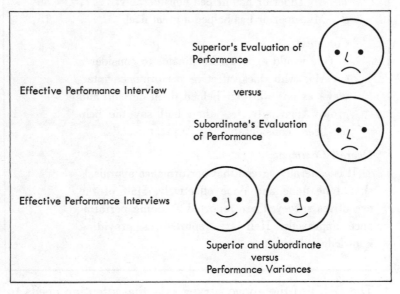

7

Performance Interview
Guidelines

A PERFORMANCE INTERVIEW was previously defined as a discussion between a superior and a subordinate about the latter's performance. It may be impromptu, it may be scheduled ahead of time. Usually, the initiative for the interview comes from the superior. It often occurs because of a dissatisfaction on the part of the superior with some aspect of the subordinate's performance.

As long as one is a manager one is faced with the challenge of conducting performance interviews. How can one's managerial effectiveness be increased by conducting performance interviews? One way is to analyze what you now do in an interview which is effective and what you now do which is ineffective. Interviewing is a skill. We learned long ago, with golf and other sports, that practice doesn't always make perfect. Practice is helpful only if you know what you are trying to master.

An analysis of many interviews, both good and bad, has led to the development of six suggestions. These six suggestions apply to any interview having to do with performance or lack of performance. These six suggestions are guidelines. They will help you in assessing where you are effective and

111

where you are ineffective in conducting performance interviews.

Let us mention the six suggestions. Then we will consider each one, in turn. The six suggestions are:

1. Coach on results.
2. Get down to cases.
3. Determine causes.
4. Make it a two-way process.
5. Set up an action plan.
6. Provide motivation.

We will need to secure a complete understanding of each suggestion, so let's consider each one more thoroughly.

COACH ON RESULTS

If I "attack" you, what will you do? Defend yourself, of course. The same reaction occurs when you "attack" a subordinate in a performance interview. Predictably, the subordinate will defend himself or herself. Let's consider some examples:

1. A manager says: "You are a poor long-range planner." This manager is criticizing the person. Another manager says: "The long-range planning in your organization is poor." This manager is stressing the result desired, namely, good long-range planning.
2. A manager says: "You are careless." Certainly, this is personal. Suppose instead the manager says: "The quality of work turned out by your organization has too many errors." Here, the manager is stressing results.

When you find it necessary to criticize, endeavor to criticize the result you are concerned about. Usually, there is a variance between what is necessary and what has been accomplished. You could express your concern, then "attack the variance, not the person."

Coaching on results doesn't mean you will avoid defensive or negative reactions altogether. It just reduces the likelihood of such reactions. This suggestion is consistent with the earlier stress on an atmosphere of approval. Coaching on results permits both superior and subordinate to jointly "attack the variance."

This suggestion reveals the critical value of having a subordinate define results he or she is going to achieve in advance. Suppose I had committed myself to my superior to improving the long-range planning six months ago, or to improving the quality of the product. Certainly, it would be easier for the superior to talk about a variance between what I committed myself to accomplish and what was accomplished. But whether targets have been set in advance or not, this suggestion is a very useful one to keep in mind.

It is particularly important to analyze your interviewing habits when you are under stress. A subordinate fails to get an important result for you. It embarrasses you with your superior. You may speak in anger. Often, at a time like this you "attack" the subordinate. Use this first suggestion as a guideline to assess the effectiveness of your interviewing skill.

GET DOWN TO CASES

Subordinates frequently comment on the generalized nature of criticism provided by their superior. The superior "hints at something." The superior "beats around the bush." In surveys conducted by Mahler Associates of more than 5,000 managers, we get the same results year after year. About one half of those surveyed report their manager is very general in talking with them about their performance.

So suggestion Number 2 is "get down to cases." Be specific

about the result. Identify the variance you are concerned about. Cite data. Provide examples. Use incidents which illustrate the result you want to see improved. Let's go back to the long-range planning illustration. The manager might well say:

> I've been concerned about the limited attention given to long-range planning in your organization. Just recently, you came to me with a rush request for equipment. You also asked for permission to work overtime. Under the emergency conditions I approved the action on both equipment and overtime. However, as I see it, the need for the equipment could have been anticipated. If it had been, it is likely we wouldn't need to be working overtime. Hence, I feel the long-range planning in your organization has been inadequate.

With this explanation, the subordinate has a much better concept of just what the manager is really concerned about.

Let's consider the second illustration used above having to do with "quality of reports." After the preliminary remarks, the manager might well use the questioning approach: "How satisfactory has the quality of our monthly reports been in the last few months?" The subordinate might well reply: "In general, I think they have been about the same as our previous months." The manager then comments: "As I look at the quality of our monthly reports, I'm not satisfied. True, the quality is about the same as previous months, but this level of quality is just not acceptable." Notice, the supervisor has shifted from talking about "quality" in general to a specific quality problem with monthly reports.

So here is a second suggestion against which to assess your interviewing skill. You can check your implementation of this skill during the course of a performance interview. Just ask subordinates to define, in their own words, what result it is that you are concerned about. The closer they come to defining it the same as you do, the better. If they don't come close, double back and talk about more specifics.

DETERMINE CAUSES

Analysis of many interviews reveals that this suggestion is most often overlooked. A manager established the fact that a variance exists. A result is not forthcoming. A problem exists. So then the manager says: "What are we going to do about it"? This "what" question bypasses the concern about causes. You might well ask why should one get concerned about causes? For several reasons. Consideration of causes makes the entire process much more of a problem-solving process. It permits exploring the need for action by subordinate, by superior, and by others. To go from a variance directly to a question: "What are you going to do about it"? gets back to personalizing the problem. We are putting the monkey on the subordinate's back. Now maybe that is where the monkey belongs. But, let's not jump to that conclusion.

Time spent exploring why a variance exists helps identify possible actions which might be taken. It increases the likelihood that the action which is taken will really reduce the variance.

When exploring causes, urge the subordinate to identify three or four possible causes. Don't reject the first one mentioned, even if you think it is an alibi. Ask for other causes. Once you have several causes on "top of the table" you can, jointly, identify those which are more important to consider and endeavor to do something about it.

Again, let's consider the "long-range planning" example. The manager says: "Why do you feel our long-range planning, particularly on equipment and manpower, is not adequate? The subordinate might well reply:

I really haven't given it the attention it deserves. Equally important, I'm not sure just how to go about doing it. How far ahead should you try to plan? How farsighted can you be, actually? Certainly, if we are going to get serious about long-range planning I'll have to get some staff help, at least part-time assistance.

Let me mention another possible cause. I can identify a need for new equipment or for more or different manpower, but if you and your superior are as conservative as you have been, we will still be talking about our long-range planning problem year after year.

Here, in short order, are four possible causes. Each suggest quite different actions. Notice that exploration of causes provides an opportunity for upward communication. It is difficult to get subordinates to share their thinking with their manager on ways the manager might change or improve. With encouragement, this type of input can be obtained during a discussion of causes. This suggestion deserves special attention because it is so often neglected.

Decision-making courses are popular today in many organizations. The big stress in rational decision making is on proper definition of the problem. This is then followed by exploring causes. Hence, the performance interview provides a rather specific opportunity for the application of rational decision making.

MAKE IT A TWO-WAY PROCESS

Stress was placed on the performance interview being a joint problem-solving process—the superior and subordinate versus the variance! To be a joint problem-solving process requires that it be a two-way process. Neither superior or subordinate should dominate the discussion.

The performance interview is often thought of as a "telling" process. The superior calls subordinates in and

1. Tells them what is wrong.
2. Tells them why it is wrong.
3. Tells them what to do about it.

This type of approach is not likely to be effective. It develops "puppets," not capable individuals. It develops resistance rather than enthusiasm for change.

Some managers find it quite natural to implement this suggestion. Some find it quite difficult to do so. In fact, some managers may not ever recognize they are completely dominating the entire interview.

The key hint for implementing this suggestion is the judicious use of questions. In the very beginning you can ask subordinates if they see the "variance" in the same way you do. You can ask them for possible actions. Two-way also means that the manager comments on the questions when such expressions are needed to insure realism governs the interview.

Let me ask you a question. How effective are you in making performance interviews a two-way, joint, problem-solving process? The more affirmative your answer to this question, the better.

SET UP AN ACTION PLAN

You can consider a performance interview effective if it leads to improved performance. To refer to a term used earlier, if the variance between the expected and the actual is reduced, the interview is effective. Here is where the fifth suggestion is so important. Setting up an action plan increases the likelihood that results will be forthcoming.

Deciding on appropriate action flows naturally from the consideration of causes. Once you have jointly identified the important cause or causes, you can begin to explore a variety of possible actions.

Implementation of this suggestion requires:

1. Considering several possible actions to correct a given cause.
2. Concentrating on one or two specific actions.
3. Being specific about who, what, and when.
4. Providing for follow-up or report back.
5. Reducing the plan to writing.

Let us refer to the previous illustration of a variance having to do with long-range planning. Four causes were identified:

1. The subordinate didn't give long-range planning sufficient attention.
2. The subordinate didn't know how to get started.
3. The subordinate hadn't made use of staff assistance.
4. The subordinate felt that asking for equipment and manpower would be rejected by higher management.

A variety of actions would grow out of these causes. Some commitment, some means of self-discipline is needed to insure adequate attention. A commitment to produce a specific long-range plan by a given date represents an effective approach. Getting advice or assistance from a staff man on technique or methodology of long-range planning also seems like a natural action to correct the second and third causes. The final cause might well be met by an agreement on the part of the superior to "go to bat" to get needed equipment and manpower once a well-documented Long-Range Plan has been prepared.

PROVIDE MOTIVATION

In Chapter 3 considerable attention was devoted to motivational theory. Now is the time and place to make practical application.

A change in behavior requires that an individual be motivated to change. You don't wait until the end of the interview to implement this suggestion. You implement it throughout the interview.

Stress the benefits to the subordinate in achieving the necessary results. The benefit has to be of consequence to the subordinate. It may be advancement, it may be an increase in compensation, it may be recognition, it may be winning in competition, it may be gaining additional responsibility or status, or it may be the sense of accomplishment gained from a job well done.

The manner in which the interview is conducted has an important impact upon the motivation of the subordinate. Much more motivation is secured if the subordinate sees it as a two-way problem-solving process. In contrast, little sustained motivation is secured from the nonconstructive, nonhelpful type of interview.

SUMMARY

We have considered six suggestions for conducting effective performance interviews. With these suggestions in mind, practice can make perfect! Well, if not perfect, at least, the suggestion will make for increased effectiveness in performance interviews.

Keep the suggestions in mind in preparing for an interview. Review them, in a self-analytical manner, after a performance interview. A checklist for doing this follows.

Such actions should lead to both increased ability and increased confidence in conducting effective performance interviews.

Performance Interview Checklist

1. *Coach on results:*
   Were results stressed or were traits stressed?
   If traits were stressed, were they related to end results?
   Was criticism personal or job centered?

2. *Get down to cases:*
   How specific were the reasons given for my opinions?
   Were specific incidents used well?
   How frank was I?

3. *Determine causes:*
   Was an attempt made to get at causes?
   Did we get at several causes?
   Did we get at the real cause(s)?

4. *Make interview a two-way process:*
   Was I dominant?
   Who did the most talking?
   Was there good give-and-take discussion?
   Were questions used to stimulate thinking?

5. *Set or reset goals or targets:*
   Were goals set against which subordinate could measure
      progress?
   Were goals specific or general?
   Were goals imposed or developed jointly?

6. *Provide motivation:*
   Did I evidence concern about subordinate?
   Did I use positive motivation?
   Was the subordinate motivated to act differently in the
      future?

8

Types of Performance Interviews

WE WILL FIND it helpful to differentiate between four different types of performance interviews. We will then suggest a process specific to each type. The four types are:

1. Progress reviews against goals.
2. Annual accomplishment reviews against goals.
3. Performance interview in absence of goals.
4. Group review of progress against goals.

Let's consider processes appropriate to each type.

PROCESS FOR PROGRESS REVIEWS AGAINST GOALS

Progress reviews are done against a set of goals. It is desirable for the superior to set the frequency of reviews when goals have been approved. A quarterly review is practically a must. It is also desirable to decide on whether to review all goals or a selected list.

The process for the progress review involves the following steps:

1. Subordinate reviews progress on all goals. During this step the discussion revolves around clarification questions and pushing for specificity. No attempt is made at

121

getting at causes. A note can be made of any causes which are commented upon in step 1.

2. Superior comments on the overall results.
3. The superior indicates the variances he or she is most concerned about.
4. The top priority variance is considered. The question to be explored thoroughly is: What are the causes? Here's a hint. Get the subordinate to talk about three or four or even more causes. Don't argue about the first one or two. They are often delightful rationalizations.

   If the subordinate doesn't do so, suggest that either or both you and the subordinate may be a cause. Once you have a set of causes, sort out the causes you should both be most concerned about.
5. Identify appropriate action to overcome the causes. You may want the action plans to be reflected in work plans.
6. Repeat the above process for variance of second priority.
7. Finally, if you haven't done so before, modify goals as necessary.

In Appendix B a case study has been presented involving a progress review against goals. The case study may be helpful in visualizing just how one might carry out the above seven steps.

PROCESS FOR ANNUAL ACCOMPLISHMENT REVIEWS AGAINST GOALS

1. The process followed in the progress review is quite appropriate for the annual accomplishment review.
2. In addition, the superior can help the subordinate "wring a year's worth of learning" from a year of experience by asking the subordinate to:

    a. Comment on what he or she had learned over the last year.

    b. Contrast successful goal achievements with unsuccessful achievements.

    c. Discuss one's effectiveness as a manager and how one might improve. This can be converted to self-improvement goals for the next year.

In Appendix B a case study of an annual performance interview has been presented. An illustration of a goals document, using responsibilities, indicators and goals, is given.

3. Attention needs to be given to any changes which need to be made in subordinate's—

    a. Responsibilities.

    b. Indicators.

    c. Goals.

4. The subordinate should be required to complete an Accomplishment Report (see Appendix B, Case D, for an example). The superior should add comments about his or her overall evaluation of the subordinate and then file the record in the subordinate's personnel file.

PROCESS FOR PERFORMANCE INTERVIEW IN THE ABSENCE OF GOALS

There may be occasions when you feel the need to have a performance interview in the absence of goals. The following process is recommended:

1. Advise the subordinate that you want to discuss a given result or condition or situation. Ask him or her to prepare for the discussion.

2. Begin by describing or defining the result you are concerned about and the reasons for your concern.

3. Discuss the present status and what would constitute a satisfactory result.
4. Discuss causes for the variance between present status and desired result.
5. Set appropriate action plans to accomplish the improvement.

GROUP REVIEW OF PROGRESS AGAINST GOALS

The progress review can be conducted in a group session. The usual setup is for an executive to conduct such a session with direct reports. Occasionally, a manufacturing manager or a regional sales manager may want to set up this "tandem" review process. The top manager and the plant manager are in the meeting. Superintendents report their progress in front of both.

We have discovered that the following process makes for effective group reviews.

1. Have direct reports give the status on the goals for their No. 1 responsibility. If you are using a restricted list of goals, have the individuals report on their No. 1 goal. Each direct report does this.
2. Repeat the process for the No. 2 and No. 3 responsibilities. Permit interruptions and clarification purposes only.
3. Ask each direct report to give the status on any other goals which would be of interest to the others.

    Caution: Do not get into a problem-solving process unless a given variance is of concern to a majority of the participants. Schedule needed problem-solving efforts restricted to those directly involved.
4. Consider any suggestions, comments, and observations that individuals want to make to be helpful to others.

5. Occasionally, a revision in a goal becomes necessary. Also a trade-off between two goals may be necessary.

Some managers conduct quarterly group sessions and hold individual sessions on an "as needed" basis.

The group process is a powerful one. It works best when there is a real need for team work.

part four

The Counseling
Interview

FEW EXECUTIVES think of themselves as counselors. Counseling is something done by specialists who have an understanding of human nature. Well, executives can avoid counseling, but they cannot avoid the problems which require counseling. A subordinate begins drinking to excess. A subordinate may begin to set a poor example in terms of absences or work hours. A subordinate may be in such a severe personal crisis it affects work performance. A subordinate may be dressing inappropriately or using language which is considered improper. Many more illustrations could be given. In some instances the situation has to do with a trivial matter. In other instances, the matter is of great consequence to all concerned.

The term counseling will be used to refer to a process whereby an executive endeavors to get a subordinate to recognize that a given behavior is inappropriate, accepts the need to change and, then, endeavors to change. A counseling interview is a two-way discussion aimed at getting a subordinate to change an inappropriate behavior.

In Chapter 9 attention will be given to a set of counseling principles. These principles are intended as guidelines when an executive plans for and conducts a counseling interview.

The guidelines also assist in self-analysis after interviews have been conducted. A specific process for conducting a counseling interview will be recommended in Chapter 10.

It is hoped that the counseling principles and process will contribute to successful counseling interviews. Counseling interviews can be considered successful when—

1. The subordinate recognizes that a behavioral change is needed.
2. Both the executive and the subordinate share in a deliberate effort to get a behavior change.
3. The deliberate effort results in a resolution of the problem. The resolution may be a behavior change, or it may be resolved by the subordinate leaving the position.
4. The subordinate respects the superior for imposing standards and for endeavoring to be helpful.

One might diagram counseling interviews as follows:

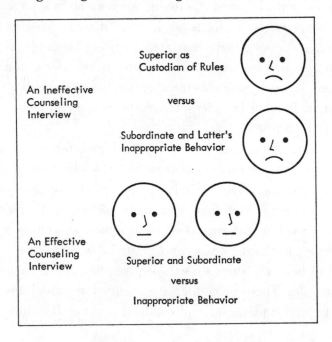

9

Counseling Principles

WE HAVE DEFINED performance interviews as those directed to job performance, whereas counseling interviews are directed toward an individual—the individual's attitude and behavior. In some instances, the two types of interview overlap. But the distinction is helpful for the basic approach differs.

Counseling begins with an attitude or behavior of the subordinate that is deemed to be inappropriate. It may be lateness, absenteeism, alcoholism, the way an individual relates with key people or customers, expense reports, influence on other personnel, or need for excessive stroking.

The subordinate may or may not realize the attitude or behavior is inappropriate. Faced with the complexities of a counseling situation, many executives choose the avoidance route. Lack of confidence, lack of experience, lack of skill, and lack of prior success experience may well justify this route. However, I believe an understanding of counseling principles and a mastery of counseling interview processes will make for a successful resolution of many counseling problems.

There is no need to fool anyone. The problems requiring counseling are complex. This complexity requires that you understand certain principles. These principles will help in planning and conducting an effective counseling process. Attention will be given to ten principles. They are:

1. Individuals can change, they can grow.
2. People under stress react negatively before they react positively.
3. A person who feels understood and accepted as he or she is now is likely to change.
4. Counseling is a learning process.
5. Counseling is not a one-time event.
6. Two types of listening are required.
7. Empathy and standards must go together.
8. Openness in communication is vital.
9. Counseling is an investment.
10. Some situations are so special or complex, referral is necessary.

Let us give further consideration to each counseling principle.

INDIVIDUALS CAN CHANGE, THEY CAN GROW

The quarterback of the football team was just an average performer until the new coach arrived. Then he blossomed into an outstanding performer. One of the reasons was that his coach didn't accept him as he was; his coach realized his untapped potential. He challenged him to perform at his optimum. The first and most fundamental principle of counseling is a belief in the possibility that individuals can change, that they can grow! In Chapter 1, attention was called to the Pygmalion effect. Here is an opportunity to get such an effect.

How often have you heard an executive say one of the following?

He isn't going to change at his age.
He is set in his ways.
She will never change.

To be effective as a counselor an executive must be optimistic about the ability of people to grow, to change. Why is this so important? Because you can't hide your attitude. People sense it if you are fatalistic about them. They sense it if you are optimistic about them. This principle relates directly to stress placed upon an atmosphere of approval in Chapter 1. You will recall this was deemed to be most crucial in an effective superior/subordinate relationship.

The basic attitude underlying counseling is essentially respect for human dignity plus an optimistic outlook. It is difficult to be effective at counseling without a truly felt respect for the individuality of the person being counseled.

PEOPLE UNDER STRESS REACT NEGATIVELY BEFORE THEY REACT POSITIVELY

The counseling process usually begins on a stressful note. The counselee is sufficiently concerned or upset to ask for a chance to talk. Or the executive is so concerned about inappropriate behavior that the executive sets up the initial discussion. In either instance, the counselee is under pressure or stress.

As likely as not, reactions of the subordinate in the early stage of the initial interview are likely to be negative. In some instances, they may be strongly negative. The critical factor is the reaction of the superior at this stage. Confronted with a strong negative reaction, the superior may well feel attacked. So the superior, in turn, attacks. A "me versus you," an "I win, you lose," situation gets underway.

This type of defensive reaction by the superior early in the session completely disrupts the implementation of the first principle. It practically dooms the counseling process to failure. Does the executive then accept the blame? Not likely. Seeing no change in behavior, the executive accepts this as confirmation of a feeling that people don't change anyhow! So we end up with two people who don't change, yet both are capable of it.

This principle should serve to alert you to the strong likelihood that you will be confronted with a negative reaction in the initial counseling interview. To use a phrase popular with the younger set, when this type of a confrontation occurs, "keep your cool."

A PERSON WHO FEELS UNDERSTOOD AND ACCEPTED AS HE OR SHE IS NOW, IS LIKELY TO CHANGE

This principle is sometimes referred to as the "happy paradox." When individuals feel understood and accepted as they are now, they become willing to change, they become less defensive. The need to be right, or to rationalize inappropriate behavior, is greatly diminished. When individuals feel understood, this enables them to take a more realistic view of their own strengths and weaknesses. They can consider their weaknesses without losing their dignity. They are not forced to a reactive protection of their security which we discussed in Chapter 1. A major goal of counseling, then, is to help a person come to see himself or herself so clearly that the need to defend oneself is reduced. The counselor strives to help counselees increase their objectivity and at the same time to more truly perceive themselves as individuals of worth.

Remember our discussion of behavioral research findings pertinent to one's self-concept in Chapter 2. Individuals have a strong need to have a concept of themselves as successful. They need to have a concept of themselves they can accept, that they feel comfortable with. Hence, a sudden or abrupt demand for a change automatically produces a negative reaction. It is threatening to the self-concept. An executive should get the subordinate being counseled to perceive limitations or inadequate behavior in terms of one's potential, and to realistically focus one's efforts so that one can modify the weaknesses and maximize strengths.

COUNSELING IS A LEARNING PROCESS

Let me ask you to explain what counseling means to you:

Having a heart-to-heart talk?
Giving fatherly advice?
Giving constructive criticism?

True counseling is really none of these things.

The object of counseling is to change the attitude and behavior of counselees by changing the thinking which has led to these attitudes and behaviors. The counseling session must be largely devoted to the counselees and an exploration of their present thinking. The counselees do not need advice and criticism, rather they need help in looking at the situation realistically. The counseling process should aim at bringing clarity and objectivity to an analysis of the inappropriate behavior or faulty attitude. It is the function of the counselor to help counselees see what the facts are—and the ultimate price which must be paid if a behavior change doesn't occur.

The ultimate price must not be stated in terms of threats or a "parents know best" attitude. The price must be expressed in relation to the subordinate's own ambitions, goals, hopes, and expectations.

Counseling involves more than providing a solution to an immediate problem. Counseling should help to produce a change in the counselee which enables the individual to make better choices in the future. It is a learning process.

COUNSELING IS NOT A ONE-TIME EVENT

It is rare that a single counseling session produces the desired change. A shorter time is required if the ineffective behavior is a mannerism or characteristic which—

1.   Is on the surface, it isn't a deep emotional thing.
2.   Has gone unrecognized by the individual.
3.   Doesn't require a major change.
4.   Doesn't require a high degree of self-discipline.
5.   Is readily seen as inappropriate.

Few problems "come in" for counseling with these fortunate characteristics. Usually the problem is complex and several sessions are required. It is wise, however, to allow enough time to elapse between sessions for the subordinate to digest what has already been discussed.

TWO TYPES OF LISTENING ARE REQUIRED

Most of us have a strong habit of listening to what is said. Some of us, of course, even find this difficult. But the real challenge in counseling comes with the ability to listen for what isn't said. Though it would seem to be simple enough, one of the most difficult tasks people face is to express how they feel. It becomes even more so when they are upset or distressed. It is essential to sort out these feelings—to get from what is said to what is meant, or what is felt. Your task is to try to understand how a troubled subordinate really feels.

One way to do this is simply to let the subordinate talk. In the course of the discussion you can see how strong the subordinate's feelings are. Let them talk it out is the familiar admonition.

You can help by labeling the feeling the subordinate is expressing without either accepting or rejecting it. For example, an employee may angrily state that the company treats employees unfairly. The executive might respond with: Are you saying that you feel the company is treating you unfairly? Subsequently, you might press further. Is it possible I've done something you think is unfair?

Two-way listening is sometimes referred to as listening between the lines. Sometimes the problem presented by the subordinate is really a substitute for other problems the subordinate finds it difficult to talk about.

EMPATHY AND STANDARDS MUST GO TOGETHER

Counseling often catches the superior in the middle. The behavior of the subordinate is inappropriate. It may be against the rules, it may adversely affect others. It may interfere with satisfactory job performance. The superior must act to fulfill his or her responsibility to the organization.

Action requires a confrontation. The confrontation may be unpleasant. This type of confrontation leads some executives to raise the question: "How can I have empathy and still enforce standards?" The answer is that you accept the individual but reject the behavior. But be sure the individual feels accepted before you get to the rejection of the behavior.

I once knew a father who used expressions such as the following with his children: "I love you dearly, but what you are now doing I dislike intensely." Obviously, you wouldn't use the same expression with a subordinate. But the implication of understanding and respect for the individual should be there as you help the individual look at behavior which is ineffective or inappropriate.

OPENNESS IN COMMUNICATIONS IS VITAL

Counseling rests upon trust and leveling. Can you express your position in a complete manner when talking to a subordinate? Does the subordinate feel free to talk with you? Many subordinates find it hard to believe that a person in authority is truly interested in them. They are unsure of the degree to which they can trust the "boss."

Openness is a real challenge to both superior and subordinate. In truth, many individuals have gone so long, in all their relations, without being open, they are fearful to even try to be open. Here is where the previous principles are so important. If the subordinates sense you have a genuine interest in them as a person, if they sense you understand them, even when you are expressing dislike for an aspect of their behavior, then the atmosphere is at least conducive to openness.

Achieving openness never comes easy. Some subordinates are so eager to please, so eager to be liked, so eager to avoid criticism, they can't reveal their underlying feelings. In some instances they can't even reveal these feelings to themselves. Other subordinates may be having difficulty trusting or liking an individual in an authority position, so they restrict their responses. Developing an ability to level, to be open, will be a real challenge to the majority of executives. Getting real openness in communication is an even tougher challenge.

COUNSELING IS AN INVESTMENT

An executive has a twofold obligation, to secure operating results and, in the process, assist those individuals in his or her organization to secure satisfaction of their needs. Some executives are concerned only about results. They are also vitally concerned about personal needs. In this case, their own! People sense this. They sense that the "boss" is only concerned about the "boss."

To assist people to satisfy their needs, in the process of getting results, does take time. It requires an investment of an executive's time. In some instances it requires a considerable investment.

In many organizations the basic policy does not permit an executive to abruptly fire an individual. This means the executive has no option but to make an investment in getting individuals with inappropriate behavior to change.

The investment is not only one of time. It also requires an emotional investment. You have to face unpleasant reactions, hostility, conflict, and other highly emotional reactions. Without realizing it, some executives shy away from the counseling investment because they are reluctant to make the emotional investment. There is a human tendency to procrastinate when facing an unpleasant and difficult confrontation with others. In effect, we choose not to make the investment of emotional strain which is anticipated. Often the confrontation turns out to have been less painful than anticipated.

SOME SITUATIONS ARE SO SPECIAL OR COMPLEX, REFERRAL IS NECESSARY

Distinguish clearly between those problems you can help with and those you cannot. This distinction is important for two reasons. First, no one can ever really solve someone else's problems—and should not take the responsibility for doing so—but it is sometimes possible to help others work out solutions to their own problems. Second, only an individual who is relatively objective can be of much help with another individual's problem-solving efforts.

The greatest difficulty individuals have in solving problems is the fact that emotion makes it hard for them to see and deal with their own problems objectively. Assistance in viewing the situation more objectively is often of real value. Objectivity is within the reach of every executive. It isn't the exclusive province of the psychologist.

Often several interviews are conducted by an executive, yet the undesirable behavior persists. The situation, in effect, becomes acute. This is a good signal to refer the individual to someone who has special training in dealing with complex behavioral-type problems. Individuals who react with excessive emotion on several occasions should be referred. Individuals who have difficulty in conversing about the situation in a consistent manner should be referred.

One special type of problem that is difficult for the executive is that of dealing with subordinates who turn to you for help in resolving strictly personal problems. The principles previously mentioned suggest the importance of evidencing interest in and concern for a subordinate. If the personal problem doesn't now nor isn't likely to adversely affect job performance, then it isn't of direct concern to the superior. After an initial exploration, it is probably best to urge the individual to secure help from someone with greater background in dealing with personal problems.

10

Counseling Interview Process

THE COUNSELING INTERVIEW process to be suggested is designed to achieve the results which should occur from an effective counseling interview—a joint effort which results in a change in behavior or attitude.

A seven-step process will be suggested. This process has been utilized by numerous executives over a period of years. The current process we started with differs considerably from the one we started with initially due to the many suggestions received from executives.

The seven steps are:

Steps	Process
1.	Do your homework.
2.	Begin by stating purpose of interview.
3.	Identify, in specific terms, the behavior or attitude you want to talk about.
4.	Stress why it is in the interest of subordinate to change.
5.	Explain a change will be necessary.
6.	Test for acceptance by asking for a plan of action.
7.	Provide for follow-up.

Let's consider each step in greater detail.

DO YOUR HOMEWORK

A considerable amount of homework is necessary. You should have sufficient data that the behavior or attitude under consideration is, in fact, occurring. Sometimes this is obvious, sometimes it isn't. It is helpful to be specific in your own mind about the behavior or attitude which is considered inappropriate. You should be able to define or state the behavior so that the subordinate will understand exactly what you are talking about.

At this point it helps to clarify just why you want the behavior to change at this time. The behavior may be at variance with established rules and regulations. The behavior may adversely reflect on the entire organization. The behavior may have an adverse effect upon personnel. In some instances the behavior or attitude is seen to have a future impact of an adverse nature upon subordinate and, possibly, the superior.

It is also possible that you desire to see a change for purely personal reasons. The behavior "bugs" you. This might be an example of a superior's idiosyncrasy. This was one type of knowledge which McGregor stressed as required for an effective superior/subordinate relationship, noted in Chapter 1.

Next in line for homework attention is the identification of the reasons it would be beneficial for the subordinate to change. A basic reason is, of course, the need to change if the subordinate desires to stay in the present position. The behavior may also have an adverse impact on opportunities for advancement and future salary increases. A change may be in order if the individual is to carry a fair share of the team effort, or if the individual is to be respected by peers. A change may be needed to set an acceptable model or example for subordinates. In some instances, behavior of an individual in one component of an organization might have an adverse impact on other components.

One admonition: *Do not devote time trying to establish the causes for the behavior.* In this respect, the counseling interview is quite unlike the performance interview. There are two reasons for this admonition. First, it is extremely difficult to get at causes. As often as not, the causes may be at a subconscious level. Second, and more importantly, it is unnecessary to get at causes. The behavior has to change no matter what the causation.

BEGIN BY STATING PURPOSE OF INTERVIEW

At the very beginning of the interview it is helpful to state the purpose. The purpose should—

1. Reflect your concern for the subordinate.
2. Establish the need to get personal.
3. Reveal your deep concern about the behavior or attitude in question.

Let's assume a subordinate has gotten in the habit of drinking too much at lunch. The interview beginning might well go like this: "I have been thinking about you for some time. There is one thing which concerns me greatly. I realize it is personal, but I feel we must talk about it. I'm concerned about the indications you are drinking too much."

IDENTIFY, IN SPECIFIC TERMS, THE BEHAVIOR OR ATTITUDE YOU WANT TO TALK ABOUT

This step is easy to suggest. It often is difficult for some executives to be specific. There is a tendency to hint about the behavior. General statements are made. The subordinate may not realize just what behavior needs to be changed. Step 3 is critical. If both parties are going to share a joint effort, then the subordinate must face the specific need to change.

Returning to the drinking at noon example, the superior

might well continue as follows: "I'm concerned about your drinking at lunch. Frankly, I have to conclude that you are having too many drinks at lunch."

Once you have stated your specific concern, stop talking. Get a reaction. Encourage the individual to talk. Remember several of the counseling principles. The subordinate is likely to react rather heatedly. Don't get into a "me versus you" type of argument. Encourage discussion about the behavior.

Returning to our example, let's assume a defensive reaction, so you can use a variety of alternatives, such as:

"Well, just review with me what happened at lunch each day last week."

"Please help me understand, why would several individuals report such behavior to me."

"If I understand what you are implying, you do admit it happens but you feel that there are no adverse consequences."

"Let's suppose the behavior is really more serious than you believe, is it wise for either you or me to ignore it?

"Obviously, I am not going to get concerned about something unless I think it is serious. It seems to me we both need to look seriously at the issue of drinking."

The upshot of step 3 should be that both the subordinate and the superior are in agreement that a behavior or attitude exists which needs to be changed. Actually, getting to this result may take several interviews.

STRESS WHY IT IS IN THE INTEREST OF THE SUBORDINATE TO CHANGE

Here's where your homework comes in. Save the strong negative of a loss of job until last. Stress more the adverse impact upon the subordinate's ambitions, reputation, and rewards. Pride is a powerful reference to use. Recall the discussion in Chapter 3 on positive and negative motivation. Stress the positive motivators before mentioning the negative ones. Don't use the threat of removal unless it is necessary to "get attention."

EXPLAIN A CHANGE WILL BE NECESSARY

It may be that the subordinate fully accepts the need for a change. Fine, step 5 has been accomplished. However, if this acceptance isn't forthcoming, it is desirable to be direct in stating that a change will be necessary and when it should take place.

Again, returning to the "drinking at noon" subordinate, let's assume there is a resistance to really face reality. A statement like this is necessary: "We have taken a good look at the problem. I have told you of my concern about your drinking too much at noon. I sense you don't share my concern. Frankly, I am going to have to ask you to stop drinking too much at noon."

TEST FOR ACCEPTANCE BY ASKING FOR A PLAN OF ACTION

During the interview you will sense agreement on the need to change, or you will reach the point of being explicit about a change being required. At this time it helps to test acceptance by asking for a plan of action. Avoid imposing your own plan. You can contrast the plans presented by the subordinate with your homework plans.

In planning action it helps to—

1. Take an immediate step.
2. Take a small one.
3. Take one which is likely to be successful.

You can then build upon the initial success by pushing on to more difficult actions. It helps to be specific about what will be done and when it will be done.

Returning to our previous example, you could ask for action planning as follows: "Now that we have agreed on the need to change, let's do two things. Please define what drinking in moderation is. One drink, fine! Now let's agree on when you will start. Monday? Fine!"

PROVIDE FOR FOLLOW-UP

The responsibility for follow-up should be placed upon the subordinate. In addition to planning the necessary action, also schedule when and in what manner the subordinate will report back to you on action taken and consequences. This step permits reinforcing successful efforts; it also helps to prevent retrogressing.

part five

The Career Discussion

EARLIER a career discussion was defined as a discussion between a superior and a subordinate about the latter's future. It might be more accurate to say the discussion is about the subordinate's future occupational situation.

You have probably noticed that the topic of advancement had a tendency to enter into discussions about performance and also counseling. The main difference, is that the primary reason for the career discussion has to do with career questions and problems. Let's put the career discussion in perspective with the other types of interviews.

Performance interviews have to do with performance. Emphasis was placed upon a variance between what was expected and what was realized. Both superior and subordinate were "problem solving the variance." They were on the same side of the table.

Counseling interviews have to do with an inappropriate behavior or attitude. The behavior could be inappropriate in terms of a negative effect upon performance, or in terms of the rules of the organization. Here again, emphasis was placed upon both the superior and subordinate jointly being concerned about the inappropriate behavior.

Career discussions provide the same joint opportunity. In

145

this case the subordinate has certain abilities. The organization has certain positions requiring a wide variety of abilities. They may need the abilities of a subordinate in the near future, they may not. The subordinate is also in competition with others. The career problem can well be thought of as a subordinate versus the requirements of a position. The superior can be of real help in assisting the subordinate to look at the requirements, to look at the probabilities of advancement, and to plan to achieve as optimum results as possible.

We will need to consider some principles pertaining specially to career discussions. These will be covered in Chapter 11. We have seen the importance of specific principles to performance and counseling interviews. They will be even more important in career discussions.

There is also need to give attention to several processes for conducting effective career discussions. One type will be exploratory. The other type will be in terms of specifications. Four alternative processes will be presented in Chapter 12.

Again, it is hoped that the combination of career discussion principles and several processes for conducting career discussions will contribute to successful career discussions. A career discussion can be considered successful when—

1. Both superior and subordinate share in a deliberate effort to be realistic about the latter's future.
2. The subordinate does become more realistic.
3. The subordinate establishes future plans which are appropriate.
4. The subordinate appreciates the interest and concern manifested by the superior.

One might diagram career discussions as follows:

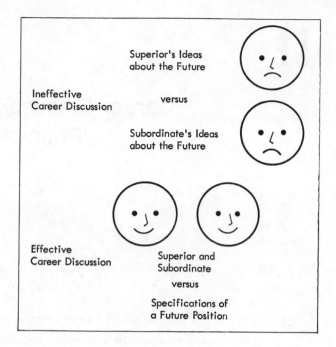

11

Career Discussion
Principles

Quite a few years ago the author asked two operating managers to participate in a demonstration career discussion. Two volunteers were selected from a group of participants. The challenge faced by the superior in the demonstration role playing was to get the subordinate to accept the fact that he or she wasn't going any further and yet be motivated to perform effectively in the subordinate's current position. The discussion went this way, abbreviated considerably:

> Boss: I called you in to talk about your future. We all reach a twilight period. You have reached yours.
> Subordinate: This is a shock. Why, I have two daughters who are about to start college.
> Boss: That's entirely irrelevant.
> Subordinate: That upsets me greatly.
> Boss: If that's the case, I'm not sure we can leave you in your present position.

As a result of this one experience I have been reluctant to urge that executives conduct career discussions unless they have received skill training. The above "boss" would certainly do much damage if he conducted actual career discussions in a like manner to his role playing.

It will be particularly important to thoroughly review the career discussion principles before endeavoring to master the processes for conducting career discussions. Nine career discussion principles will be listed, followed by a thorough discussion of each.

CAREER DISCUSSION PRINCIPLES

1. Almost all individuals have a strong concern about their future.
2. Managers, at all levels, want to talk about their future with their superior. The same managers are reluctant to talk with their subordinates about their future.
3. It is not necessary or desirable to tell individuals they will or will not be promoted.
4. A primary outcome of a career discussion should be an increase in realism.
5. Career discussions should assist individuals to look at themselves in terms of the requirements of higher positions.
6. Career discussions are more productive if they precede critical decisions.
7. A career discussion is important in developing future talent, in motivating talent which is not going any higher, and in avoiding obsolescence.
8. Career discussions are a tangible indication of concern for a subordinate.
9. Executives who have a reputation for furthering the careers of their subordinates, have an advantage in attracting and keeping top talent.

FURTHER CONSIDERATION OF CAREER DISCUSSION PRINCIPLES

Almost All Individuals Have a Strong Concern about Their Future

In survey after survey, employees at all levels of the organization report that it is very important for them to have an opportunity to advance. Two out of three say it is "very important." Only 6 percent do not say advancement is important. It is very rare that individuals indicated a lack of career concern. How often do subordinates get a chance to talk about the future with their superior? We have considerable survey data on this question. The survey results have been secured from more than 5,000 subordinates. Superiors have ranged from presidents to second-level supervisors.

Has your superior discussed your ambitions, your aspirations for the future with you?   *Percent*

a. My superior has not done so.............................. 27
b. My superior has rarely done this......................... 23
c. My superior has done this now and then................. 45
d. My superior has done this quite often..................... 5

It appears that there is a 50 percent chance of having a discussion of one's ambitions with a superior.

How often does your superior talk with you about future opportunities for persons like yourself?   *Percent*

a. My superior has never done this.......................... 26
b. My superior rarely does this.............................. 21
c. My superior does this now and then...................... 50
d. My superior does this quite often........................ 3

Again, the odds are about one out of two of having a talk about future opportunities with a superior.

Has your superior discussed with you specific things which you might do to better qualify yourself for taking on greater responsibilities in the future?	Percent
a. My superior hasn't had such a discussion with me........	34
b. My superior has rarely done this..........................	21
c. My superior has done this now and then..................	39
d. My superior has done this quite often....................	6

There is less than a 50 percent chance of having a discussion with one's boss about specific things which you need to do better to get ahead.

Has your superior encouraged you to do anything specifically to better prepare yourself for taking on greater responsibilities in the future?	Percent
a. My superior has never done this..........................	31
b. My superior has rarely done this..........................	23
c. My superior has done this on occasion....................	41
d. My superior has done this quite often....................	5

Still the same high odds against getting help from a superior.

To what extent has your superior told you of the requirements you might well be expected to meet to qualify for larger responsibilities in the future?	Percent
a. My superior has not explained them at all................	44
b. My superior has explained them in general terms........	40
c. My superior has explained them in some detail...........	13
d. My superior has explained them quite thoroughly........	3

This activity appears to be almost nonexistent.

How satisfied are you with the opportunities you see ahead for advancement in this organization?	Percent
a. I am dissatisfied with prospects of advancement..........	15
b. I am somewhat dissatisfied with prospects of advancement..	31
c. I am satisfied with prospects of advancement.............	44
d. I am quite satisfied with prospects for advancement........	10

Imagine, nearly one out of two individuals are dissatisfied with their prospects of advancement.

How specific are the actions which have been planned to help you prepare for taking on greater responsibilities in the future?	Percent
a. This hasn't been done	42
b. This has been done in general terms	39
c. One or two specific actions have been planned	16
d. Three or more specific actions have been planned	3

Again, a practically nonexistent activity.

In discussing factors impacting upon satisfactory performance in Chapter 2, mention was made of a formula, R/N, indicating an executive was responsible for securing results and, in the process, providing for the need satisfaction of those involved. One need, common to most of us, is to progress in one's chosen area of endeavor. Managers are certainly concerned about their careers. So are subordinates at each level of an organization.

This concern means that it is quite unlikely that an executive can avoid career discussions for long. At some time confrontation on career questions must be faced.

If advancement is one of the more important needs of our employees, then we must be skillful in taking this into account as we seek to motivate performance and to retain capable personnel in the organization.

Managers Want to Talk about Their Future with Their Superior; Same Managers Are Reluctant to Talk with Their Subordinates about Their Future

In survey after survey, managers indicate that they would like to talk with their superior about their careers. This is true at all levels of management. Yet seldom, if ever, have they had such a discussion with their subordinates. Why this strange paradox? Why don't managers do unto others as they would have others do unto them?

Several reasons probably account for this strange situation. One is a misconception about what a career discussion is. Managers often expect subordinates to want to know definitely about their advancement opportunities. Since they are either unable or unwilling to be precise, managers avoid having a discussion. Other managers avoid such discussions because they don't know how to do it in an effective manner. In some instances, the situation is a delicate one. Some managers are uncertain about their own next move. It is even worse if they sense they are not going to move. Discussions with a subordinate about the latter's future can certainly be difficult under such circumstances.

Career discussions are most likely to be avoided when the manager knows that the subordinate is not likely to be able to move, either because of lack of opportunity or because of lack of competitive abilities. Later, principles will be devoted to some ways to overcome the normal resistance to career discussions. The career discussion suggestions, to be given later, also will assist in developing both skill and confidence, both of which are needed to assist in overcoming resistance to career discussions.

It Is Not Necessary or Desirable to Tell Individuals They Will or Will Not Be Promoted

Survey results were given to a top-level executive. They showed that each of his subordinates wanted to have a career discussion. The executive said, "Why, one man is 64. What questions could he have? In any case, I'm not going to tell a man he will be promoted. Neither am I going to tell him that he will not be promoted. So, what would we talk about? I don't think a career discussion is necessary."

The executive well illustrated the importance of this principle. It is not desirable to tell individuals they will be promoted until a decision has been made and the move is about to be made. To promise a promotion is dangerous, since final decisions are always made at one or more levels above a given executive. The subordinate knows that the best an executive can do is give a strong recommendation. Of course, subordinates would not be displeased to be told that they will be promoted. But, they would be greatly upset if a promised promotion went to someone else. So we would argue that it is not necessary to tell individuals they will be promoted.

It is undesirable to tell individuals they will never be promoted. Slamming the door, with finality, isn't desirable. It certainly doesn't help sustain motivation to continue to perform well. In addition, even though the odds are extremely long, an individual should be left with some hope. Occasionally, we have seen surprisingly long odds eventually come through. It is also unnecessary to tell individuals they will never be promoted. In the next principle we will suggest that there is merit in individuals beginning to look at the probabilities somewhat realistically. It helps them plan their relationship with a given organization. It also influences one's external decisions pertaining to such things as standard of living, pursuit of educational opportunities, and retirement.

We have stressed two things one need not do in a career discussion. This still leaves plenty of room to implement the other career discussion principles.

A Primary Outcome of a Career Discussion Should Be an Increase in Realism

This is a most important principle. It defines one critical outcome to be achieved in a career discussion. The executive isn't telling subordinates they will or will not be promoted. The executive is assisting subordinates to look at their career situations in an objective manner, in a realistic manner.

A subordinate can benefit from knowing the requirements or specifications that management considers in making appointments. An executive can share this knowledge with a subordinate. True, in some instances, the superior may have to ferret out this type of data.

Subordinates can benefit from an analysis of their assets and liabilities in relation to the requirements. Here an executive can do two things: Encourage subordinates to analyze themselves against the specifications, and also help subordinates by sharing his or her own assessments of present abilities and liabilities of the subordinate versus the specifications.

There are two other types of questions which it is difficult to be precise about. How likely are openings going to occur? How tough is the competition? Past experience may permit the executive to make certain observations. If the executive has some basis for providing an input on these two questions, fine. If not, this opportunity to assist the subordinate in being realistic will have to be passed.

Notice that this principle puts the superior and subordinate on the same side of the table. Both looking, as realistically as possible, at abilities versus specifications, and abilities versus competition.

Career Discussions Should Assist Individuals to Look at Themselves in Terms of the Requirements of Higher Positions

An executive can help subordinates by advising them of the more important requirements or specifications which management considers in making appointments. A checklist of the more frequently used requirements has been given in Chapter 6. In some instances it will be necessary for the executive to do some "homework" prior to the career discussion.

Once subordinates know the requirements, a second step can be taken—that of looking objectively at the extent to which they currently meet the requirements. Self-analysis should be encouraged. Subordinates can benefit from an understanding of how their own self-analysis compares with that of their supervisor.

It is difficult to avoid a superior versus subordinate discussion at this point. The challenge is for both parties to look as objectively as possible at the abilities versus the requirements.

The third step is a natural one, an action plan to overcome liabilities and strengthen assets, wherever this type of effort makes sense.

Career Discussions Are More Productive if They Precede Critical Decisions

Try to talk calmly with individuals who are upset because they have just missed out on a promotion. It isn't likely to be an objective or a productive discussion. However, if career discussions are avoided, then they inevitably take place at critical decision times.

So, an investment in career discussions should be made when critical decisions are not imminent. Subordinates who either have an opportunity to go to a higher level job, or *believe* they have, can benefit from a career discussion. Individuals who are not on top of their current position will, of course, be getting performance interviews, not career discussions. Individuals who are not likely to go further, and who have accepted this, do not need a career discussion unless avoiding obsolescence is a potential need.

A Career Discussion Is Important in Developing Future Talent, in Motivating Talent Which Is Not Going Any Higher, and in Avoiding or Overcoming Obsolescence

A career discussion can help individuals identify strengths and weaknesses early in their careers so they can begin to do something about them. These discussions help assure a continuity of talent and increase the likelihood of getting people to reach their optimum level of effectiveness.

Some observers of business organizations say that companies promote individuals up and up, until they fail. Going one step too far can be a disaster for both the individual and the organization. We noted five basic factors contributing to our feeling successful and, hence, being motivated in Chapter 6. Individuals had to be in jobs in which they were capable to qualify for any of these factors. So career discussions can help individuals gracefully accept the likelihood that they aren't going any higher. It can help them to gain other satisfactions, to offset the prospect of limited future progress.

Career Discussions Are a Tangible Indication of Concern for a Subordinate

If time goes by and no one talks to you about your career, the vacuum gets filled with anxiety. You may assume you have no future. At this point the grass may seem greener somewhere else. So your one and only career discussion may well be an exit interview!

Many executives have found that periodic career discussions, particularly with impatient individuals, have resulted in their taking a longer time perspective.

One doesn't have career discussions just to minimize turnover. However, reduced turnover is a "fallout" benefit as often as not.

Executives Who Have a Reputation for Furthering the Careers of Their Subordinates, Have an Advantage in Attracting and Keeping Top Talent

Career discussions which lead to self-development action and to appropriate placements and transfers can yield a dividend to the executive. The executive develops a reputation as an executive who moves his subordinates, who develops subordinates, who pushes them up.

Sure, good subordinates keep leaving for other spots in the organization. But, one's reputation begins to be an advantage in attracting and keeping top talent.

You can recall such executives in your own experience. So career discussions help the subordinate, they help the organization, and they help the superior. Let's begin to do more of them and do them effectively!

12

Career Discussion
Alternatives

IN THIS CHAPTER attention will be given to four career discussion alternatives. It will be necessary to get a "feel" for what is likely to happen in each alternative. Then you can select the one or ones which seem most appropriate for a given situation. The four alternatives are:

1. Exploratory discussion in terms of one's current position.
2. Exploratory discussion in terms of future positions.
3. Career discussion in terms of a specification for a general position level.
4. Career discussion in terms of a specification for a given position.

EXPLORATORY DISCUSSION IN TERMS OF ONE'S CURRENT POSITION

This alternative involves the use of a set of questions. The superior asks the subordinate to prepare answers to these questions and then come in for a thorough discussion of the answers. A worksheet made up of these questions appears on pages 160–62.

In preparation for the career discussion it is helpful for the superior to review the subordinate's answers in advance.

Notes can be made of areas of disagreement and of areas needing further exploration.

The recommended discussion sequence is as follows:

1. Superior states purpose of the discussion. Stress is placed on thinking, talking, and, where necessary, planning with regard to the subordinate's future.
2. The subordinate is encouraged to discuss the answers given to the questions on the worksheet. It helps to have the subordinate comment on all questions before getting into a thorough discussion of any one answer.
3. Once the subordinate has reveiwed answers to all the questions, a thorough discussion should take place. Give particular attention to areas of disagreement.
4. Specific plans of action should be prepared after the exploratory discussion by the subordinate.

Exploratory Career Discussion
(current position)

This set of questions has been designed to give you an opportunity to discuss those aspects of your position which are of most interest and importance to you. Please feel free to express how you view your present assignment.

Thus it is hoped that you can be assisted not only in setting realistic goals, but also in attaining them. The value of this information depends on the frankness and care with which you answer the questions.

_____

Name

_____

Date completed

---

1. Do you feel that you have an adequate understanding of the requirements of your position? On which of your position responsibilities would a clearer understanding be helpful?

2. With most positions there are some things we like and some things we don't like. What are some of the things you like most about your position? Like least?

3. What phases of your work do you feel you do best?

4. Do you find there is an opportunity in your work to do those things which you do best?

5. Looking at your position as a whole, what would you say you have learned in the past year?

6. Looking at your position as a whole, what would you say you have contributed in the past year?

7. Are there any parts of your position on which you feel you want more experience or training?

8. What changes do you think should be made which would help you do your current position better or more easily? (Consider such things as instruction, communications, procedures, cooperation of others, supervision received, etc.)

9. Do you feel your position gives you an opportunity to learn things which are useful in preparing you for another position? If not, what suggestions do you have?

10. Do you have any other comments or suggestions that you wish to make about your position and your future here?

EXPLORATORY DISCUSSION IN TERMS OF FUTURE POSITIONS

This alternative is similar in process to the first alternative. However, the questions all pertain to the future. The superior suggests that the subordinate prepare answers to the questions and then come in for a thorough discussion. It is helpful, in preparation, to review the answers to the questions. One can note areas for full exploratory discussions.

The same discussion sequence suggested for the first alternative is appropriate here:

1. The superior can help greatly by assisting the subordinate to view the future with realism.

2. The superior should get a good "feel" for the subordinate's ambitions and interests.
3. You might very well discuss the requirements to be met.
4. You may, further, observe the extent to which you feel the subordinate meets the requirements.
5. Any important "gaps" calls for planning some specific developmental action, and then implementing the plans.

Exploratory Career Discussion
(future positions)

This form has been designed to give you an opportunity to discuss those aspects of your future which are of most interest and importance to you. Please feel free to express how you view your immediate and long-range plans.

In this way you can be assisted in setting realistic goals for the future. The value of this information depends on the frankness and care with which you answer the questions.

Name

Date completed

---

1. How do you feel about your career progress to date?

2. What is the next position you hope to fill in the organization?

3. Realistically, you are in competition for promotional opportunities. You have some competitive advantages, you
have some competitive disadvantages. What do you believe
them to be:

   Advantages   *Disadvantages*

4. What can be done to overcome or minimize the disadvantages?

5. It sometimes helps to think longer range about one's career. For example, what kind of work do you hope to be
doing five years from now?

6. How can you best prepare so that you can achieve your
ambitions?

7. Are there any considerations, such as location, change in
location, amount of traveling, family situation which need
to be taken into account over the next five years?

CAREER DISCUSSION IN TERMS OF A SPECIFICATION FOR A GENERAL POSITION

This type of career discussion is oriented around the aspiration to reach a given level position. The position level
may be one such as a plant manager level or a general

manager level position. Usually the position is two or more moves down the road. Specifications can be used but they are general ones, ones which refer to given level. An example of a set of specifications for a plant manager follows. In the fourth alternative to be considered next, we will make use of a specification prepared for a specific position.

Specifications for a
Plant Manager Level Position

1. Must have had experience in two or more major sub-functions, such as production, quality control, material, and maintenance.

2. Should have had experience in both union and nonunion plants, with negotiation experience.

3. A record of having obtained quite satisfactory operating results.

4. Demonstrated ability to secure the cooperation of an entire plant in getting needed results.

5. Willing to live in remote locations.

6. Willing to move every four to six years.

7. Knowledgeable of manufacturing processes.

8. Strongly cost oriented, business oriented.

9. Ability to select and develop a strong supervisory and management team.

10. Relates effectively with other departments, with suppliers and customers.

The first step in using this alternative is the preparation of general specifications. In some organizations such documents already exist. If they do not, it will be necessary to prepare one like the above example.

The second step is to discuss the general specifications with the subordinate to insure a full understanding exists.

The third step involves both superior and subordinate evaluating how well the subordinate meets the specifications. A response scale such as the following can be used:

FM—Fully meets.
NM—Nearly meets, minor exception or reservation.
PM—Partially meets, important reservations.
DM—Doesn't meet at the present time.

The fourth step involves a discussion of the similarities and differences in the initial evaluations. Differences need to be talked over and resolved. This discussion should identify two or three situations where improvement is deemed to be both desirable and necessary. This then leads to step five. Step five calls for the preparation of an appropriate plan of action, preferably with a time schedule.

CAREER DISCUSSION IN TERMS OF A SPECIFICATION FOR A GIVEN POSITION

In this type of discussion a specific position is under consideration. It is likely that a previous discussion has revealed a strong interest on the part of a subordinate for a specific position. Often this is the executive's own position.

Preparation

The executive should identify the more important specifications or requirements for the position in question. It is an advantage to talk over the specifications with one's own superior before the career discussion. It also helps to prepare an assessment as to the specifications which are met, in the executive's opinion, and those which are not currently met. It is also helpful to ask the subordinate to do the same.

Discussion Sequence

The suggested sequence for discussion with the subordinate follows:

1. Review position requirements for the position under consideration.
2. Ask the subordinate to report on the extent to which the requirements are met.
3. Share your evaluation on how well the individual meets the requirements. Encourage the subordinate to accept your evaluation or provide evidence in subsequent performance to change your evaluation.
4. If it is appropriate for the subordinate to make a serious effort to correct any "gaps," then prepare a specific plan of action, with a time schedule.
5. If it doesn't seem appropriate, stress the importance of the current position, the opportunity to make a bigger contribution in the same position, and the need to avoid obsolescence.

part six

The Removal Interview

A REMOVAL INTERVIEW is an interview in which the superior has the unpleasant task of advising the subordinate that the latter can no longer remain in his or her present position. If you made the original appointment, then the removal interview is tacit admission that you made a mistake. As often as not, you can take solace in the fact that you inherited somebody else's mistake.

The removal interview, hopefully, has been preceded by a combination of performance interviews, counseling interviews, and career discussions. In spite of this effort, the needed results or changes are not forthcoming, so removal from the position has to occur. You will recall in the discussion of the importance of a position, Chapter 2, we stressed the fact that: (1) a position must be needed, and (2) the incumbent must perform satisfactorily.

The removal interview is often postponed for months because the task is an unpleasant one. It is impossible to set any guidelines on how patient one should be. However, if the above interviews are done with skill and the results are not forthcoming, then an adverse decision must be made.

Chapter 13 considers the removal decision, and attention is given to the process of the removal interview in Chapter 14.

An effective removal interview has been conducted when:

1. The interviewee fully understands he or she can no longer remain in the position.
2. A time schedule has been established.
3. The superior has agreed to be helpful in the transition to be made by the subordinate.

No matter what you do you can't make the removal interview a pleasant process. Neither can you avoid shock to the subordinate. The subordinate may even have been somewhat apprehensive. Receiving the final word is still a shock. Neither should you expect, at this late date, to counsel. Hopefully, you can part company without acrimony or resentment. A removal interview might be diagrammed as follows:

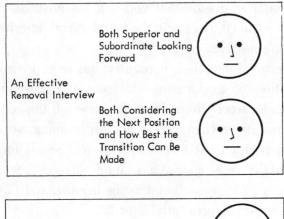

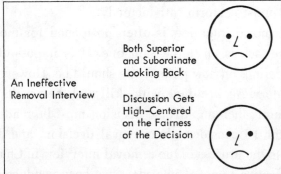

13

The Removal Decision

THE REMOVAL DECISION may become necessary for quite different reasons. In some instances, a given position is no longer needed. Admittedly, this is rare. More frequently, the removal decision is required because the incumbent is not performing at a satisfactory level. In this latter situation, two variations occur frequently. In one situation the individual does become a victim of the Peter Principle. He or she does get promoted a level above their competence. In a second situation the individual has been in a given position for some time. The title stays the same but the requirements change drastically. We usually refer to these individuals as being victims of obsolescence.

Removal may also be necessary, on rare occasions, because of gross misconduct. Other reasons could be mentioned. The appropriate approach will vary with the reason for removal and the attendant circumstances. The approach will also vary depending upon the individual's past contribution, level, and length of service.

Let's consider the decision process for each of the above reasons.

THE MISCONDUCT DECISION

This decision is usually made when the misconduct is discovered. Little needs to be said in the way of an approach to the decision. A word of caution needs to be given. The evidence of misconduct should be solid. On decisions such as this, which are likely to be abrupt, it is desirable to talk to two types of staff resources, the personnel officer and the legal officer. Obviously, higher levels of management must also be involved in the final decision.

THE "ELIMINATION OF THE POSITION" REMOVAL

The elimination of a position usually occurs as a part of an organizational study. Often an entire level is eliminated. This decision is primarily a structural one. The performance or abilities of the incumbent are not in question. The approach to this decision is usually influenced by the nature of the organizational study. There is a secondary decision involved. Will the individual be offered another position in the organization or will it be necessary for the individual to leave the organization. This staffing question should, of course, be answered as a part of the organizational study.

THE "NONPERFORMANCE" DECISION

The decision should have been preceded by performance interviews or counseling interviews. Let us assume the "dynamics and the mechanics" of these interviews were carried out fully. One must then conclude a serious effort was made to get the desired improvement and it was not forthcoming. Therefore, removal is justified and will be necessary.

Some executives have found the following process to be helpful in making the final decision.

1. Preparation of a set of specifications. In effect, you are doing a retroactive selection process. You might call it a deselection process. In Chapter 4 we suggested several types of specifications. A "short" or "intermediate" type is appropriate to use for this purpose.
2. Assess how well the incumbent meets the specifications. It is helpful to have one's superior do this and also a knowledgeable staff officer. An example of a convenient worksheet is shown in Exhibit 13–1 and a completed worksheet is given in Exhibit 13–2.
3. The last step is to make a final decision. It is necessary to weigh some specifications more than others. Some specifications are an absolute necessity, others are desirable but not that critical. The analysis process, with multiple-inputs, should enable the executive to come to a final decision that is fair to all concerned.

Some executives make use of goals in arriving at the removal decisions. An example of a goals document, which can be used for this purpose is found in Appendix B, Case D on pages 204–13.

The superior evaluates the extent to which the goals have been accomplished. This evaluation can be reviewed with other knowledgeable executives to insure objectivity. The process doesn't make the decision but it does provide meaningful data that facilitates arriving at an objective decision. The data also encourages more timely decision making.

In summary, the removal decision is usually a difficult one. A removal may be made for gross misconduct, for obsolescence, or for nonperformance. Use of specifications or goals as a reference helps in making the final decision. A negative decision calls for a final removal interview. A suggested process for doing this is presented in the next chapter.

EXHIBIT 13–1

QUALIFICATIONS
WORKSHEET

Name	Position

Prepared by	Date

Important specifications: *Analysis:*

1.   1.

2.   2.

3.   3.

4.   4.

5.   5.

6.   6

7.   7.

Interpretation for analysis:
+ Fully meets specifications.
√ Meets, minor reservations.
– Doesn't now meet, might in future.
– – Doesn't now meet, not likely to do so in future.

EXHIBIT 13–2

QUALIFICATIONS WORKSHEET

George Jones	*General Manager— Div. A*
Name	Position
Ray Smith *Group Vice President*	*7/31*
Prepared by	Date

Important specifications:	*Analysis·*
1. Tough-minded and demanding	−−
2. Skillful in negotiating with customers, suppliers, and union	−
3. Experience on several functions in this type of business	+
4. Ability to select and develop a management team	−
5. Experienced in doing business off shore	+
6. Good grasp technical aspects of the business	+
7. Willing to work in big city	+

Interpretation for analysis:
+ Fully meets specifications.
/ Meets, minor reservations.
− Doesn't now meet, might in future.
−− Doesn't now meet, not likely to do so in future.

14

The Removal Interview

IN THIS CHAPTER we will review a process to be used when the decision to remove an individual has been made due to non-performance or obsolescence. The approach to use in a gross misconduct-type situation is sufficiently straightforward that no suggestions will be provided for this type of interview. It will be assumed that the suggestions given in the prior chapter on the removal decision have been made. In this interview you want to be sure the incumbent recognizes that he or she can no longer remain in the position. Looking ahead, you want to be as helpful as possible in the subordinate's transition to another position. You also have to avoid discouraging or demoralizing the individual by stressing negatives.

It is most important you do not use the removal interview for further counseling. It is desirable to schedule the interview so it will be uninterrupted. It helps to do it near the end of the afternoon. The interview will come as a shock. It makes it easier for the subordinate to be able to leave the office shortly after the interview. Let's consider the removal interview process.

176

REMOVAL INTERVIEW PROCESS

The sequence of the interview involves the following steps:

1. Make your initial statement. It should go something like this: "For two individuals to work together, I think you would agree, confidence must exist on both sides. Try as hard as I can, I can't develop the confidence in you I would like to have. Therefore, it will be necessary to remove you from your present position."

2. The reaction is likely to be a request for additional reasons. Don't add any further explanation. Repeat your initial statement. Allow that the reasons for lack of confidence may well be primarily yours. You could probably add specific details as to reasons but they are inappropriate at this point. You have passed the remedial stage. To list critical negatives at this point is of no avail. It both angers and depresses the subordinate. It doesn't help in the transition. The initial statement permits the subordinate to explain the removal as a "chemistry" problem.

3. Shift over to future planning. Establish the ground rules on the schedule. The timing is such an individual thing, no suggestions are really pertinent. However, it helps to be precise about the date the subordinate will be removed from the payroll.

    Encourage the subordinate to prepare a plan of action for making the transition. Offer to be helpful. It is desirable to agree on the statement you will give on "reasons for leaving" to potential employees. Don't plan too much in this initial session.

4. Remember your initial statement will come as a shock. Individuals react quite differently to shock. Some become angry. They make extreme statements. Some become

hurt. Some may become upset. There isn't much you can say at this point to prevent this shock. You can help by taking a friendly, helpful approach. You can help by not getting defensive or, otherwise, reacting to any hostility displayed by the subordinate.

5. Provide encouragement and assistance at periodic intervals after the initial removal interview. One thing seems to be true. When an individual shifts from a position where he or she is not performing to one where performance is satisfactory, the travail of the removal interview and subsequent search for a new position all fade into distant memory for all concerned.

6. Recognize also that you are likely to be dealing with a strong guilt feeling on your own part. This guilt often leads you to say and do things which are inappropriate. The statements or actions may relieve your guilt but they usually don't really help the subordinate with his or her transition.

Here are some classic "no-no's":

1. Don't tell the individual that removal is for his or her own good.

2. Don't tell the individual that he or she will feel much better later.

3. Don't tell the individual that he or she will be better off elsewhere.

4. Don't tell the individual you would like to leave also.

5. Don't tell the individual your superior feels the same way you do. If the individual so desires, do arrange for an interview with your superior.

part seven

Bibliography

THE BIBLIOGRAPHY is divided into two sections. The numbered references that appear in Part One are given for their respective chapters. These are followed by additional references for each Part which are considered to be of practical value. The additional references provide a greater depth of coverage than could be accomplished in a book devoted to such varied types of interviewing.

NUMBERED REFERENCES

Chapter 1

1. McGregor, Douglas. *The Human Side of Enterprise.* New York: McGraw-Hill, 1960.
2. McGregor, Douglas. "Conditions of Effective Leadership In The Industrial Organization," *Journal of Consulting Psychology,* 1944, 8, 55–63.
3. McGregor, Douglas. "Conditions of Effective Leadership In The Industrial Organization," *Journal of Consulting Psychology,* 1944, 8, 55–63.

Chapter 2

1. Roe, Anne. *The Psychology of Occupations.* John Wiley & Sons: New York, 1956.

2. Maslow, A. H. *Motivation and Personality*. New York: Harper, 1954.
3. Terkel, Studs. *Working*. New York: Pantheon Books, 1972.
4. Gellerman, Saul W. *Motivation and Productivity*. New York: American Management Association, 1963.

Chapter 3

1. Mahler, Walter R. *Diagnostic Studies*. Reading, Mass.: Addison-Wesley, 1973.
2. Herzberg, F., Mausner, B., and Snyderman, B. *The Motivation to Work*. 2d ed. New York: Wiley, 1959.
3. Livingston, Sterling. "Pygmalion in Management," *Harvard Business Review*, July–August 1969, pp. 81–88.

ADDITIONAL REFERENCES

Part One: Pertinent Behavior Research.

Leavitt, Harold J. *Managerial Psychology*. 2d ed. Chicago: University of Chicago Press, 1964.
Leavitt devotes seven chapters to deepening insight into individuals. His chapter on assessment is pertinent to the selection challenge stressed in Part Two of this book. Leavitt devotes seven chapters to interpersonal relationships. Several of these chapters are directly relevant to the interviews covered in this book.

Levinson, Harry. *The Exceptional Executive*. Cambridge, Mass.: Harvard University Press, 1968.
The author talks about what the organization and work mean to people. Within a framework of psychoanalytic theory, he stresses three basic managerial tasks. The reader will gain increased understanding of the complexities of superior-subordinate interactions.

Nosow, Sigmund, and Form, William H. *Man, Work and Society*. New York: Basic Books, Inc., 1962.

Five articles are devoted to the meaning of work. Attention is also devoted to career patterns, to social status of occupations, to occupational mobility, and to personal adjustment to the world of work.

Stogdill, Ralph M. *Handbook of Leadership.* New York: The Free Press, 1974.

An authoritative review of the research literature on leadership. Two chapters are devoted to leadership traits, one to factor analysis of leadership characteristics.

Varela, Jacobo A. *Psychological Solutions to Social Problems.* New York: Academic Press, 1971.

An attempt is made to apply recent psychological theory to problems such as selection, performance appraisal, counseling, and other such business problems. Theory is introduced through the use of examples of actual applications.

Vroom, Victor H. *Work and Motivation.* New York: Wiley, 1964.

Vroom propounds on a basic theory for relating motivation and work. Complex but worth the effort.

Part Two: The Selection Challenge

Dooker, Joseph. Ed. *Selection of Management Personnel.* Vols. 1 and 2. New York: American Management Association, 1957.

An old book but one with many practical articles and case studies.

Kahn, Robert L., and Channell, Charles. *The Dynamics of Interviewing.* New York: Wiley, 1957.

An old book but unique. It stresses both the theory and practice of interviewing. The psychological basis of the interview is explored. Techniques for effective interviewing are covered. Interviewing, as used in this book, covers much more than the employment interview.

Peter, L. F., and Hull, Raymond. *The Peter Principle.* New York: Morrow, 1969.

In spite of its humorous side, a provocative book. The challenge to avoid rising to a level of incompetence is of consequence to both the superior making the appointment and the subordinate who is appointed.

Varela, Jacoba A. *Psychological Solutions to Social Problems*. New York: Academic Press, 1971.

Provides interesting illustrations of the application of behavioral research findings to business problems. Goes far beyond the common-sense approach.

Part Three: The Performance Interview

Drucker, Peter. *The Effective Executive*. New York: Harper & Row, 1967.

This is the type of book you ask a subordinate to read in hopes he or she may become more effective.

Kellogg, Marion S. *What to Do about Performance Appraisal*. New York: American Management Association, 1965.

Kellogg devotes several chapters to coaching appraisal (her term for performance appraisal). Many practical suggestions are provided. A very readable, helpful reference.

————. *When Man and Manager Talk—A Casebook*. Houston: Gulf Publishing Company, 1969.

Stresses the value of being more formal, more deliberate in talking about work expectations and about performance, salary, and career discussions. The book contains many practical suggestions.

Part Four: The Counseling Interview

Kellogg, Marion S. *Closing the Performance Gap*. New York: American Management Association, 1967.

Kellogg emphasizes what is needed for real development to take place. Stress is placed on the importance of work itself and the overall climate. Many practical suggestions are given to help a manager think through the challenge of assisting subordinates to develop.

Lovin, Bill C., and Casstevens, E. R. *Coaching, Learning and Action*. New York: American Management Association, 1971.

This book is a practical aid for individuals who do on-the-job coaching. Considerable attention is given to adult learning, followed by several chapters on coaching tactics and strategies.

Mager, R. F., and Pipe, Peter. *Analyzing Performance Problems,* Belmont, California: Fearon, 1970.
An interesting and readable booklet on the problems that arise because individuals are not doing what they are supposed to do. A series of questions are recommended to be used when faced with a "performance problem." Useful even though illustrations pertain to educational situations.

Part Five: The Career Discussion

Kellogg, Marion S. *Career Management.* New York: American Management Association, 1972.
A provocative argument for career management as a joint, co-equal process between an individual and the employing organization. Kellogg make obsolete many traditional approaches to manpower planning.

Super, Donald E. *The Psychology of Careers.* New York: Harper & Row, 1957.
A comprehensive study of career patterns and life stages. Provides valuable insight into a complex phenomena.

Appendixes

Appendix A
Skill Training in the
Selection Interview

IN OUR EXPERIENCE, skill in selection interviewing is developed primarily by conducting interviews with the approach suggested in Chapter 5 and in Chapter 6. Preparatory instruction is helpful. A one-day learning module has proven itself. The agenda for the one-day program follows:

Unit	Subject	Time
1.	The selection process. (Lecture/discussion using the material from Chapter 4.)	1 hr.
2.	The selection interview. Questions provided in Chapter 5 are discussed.	1 hr.
3.	The selection decision. Material covered in Chapter 6 is presented and discussed.	1 hr.
4.	Practice interviews (first half). Participants are set up in pairs. One is designated an interviewer, one an interviewee. A likely position is selected for which the interviewee might be a possible candidate.	2 hrs.

A brief specification is prepared (6–10 specifications).

The interviewer is asked to complete the questions pertaining to accomplishments (See No. 1 through 16 in Chapter 6). Set a 40-minute schedule for this.

Unit	*Subject*	*Time*
	Upon completion of these questions, both partners, independently, note the extent to which the specifications are met. They then compare notes. The interviewee then comments upon the interviewer's use of questions.	
	The two partners then reverse roles and repeat the above process.	
5.	The selection interview (second half).........	2 hrs.
	Roles are once more reversed. The interviewee is asked to complete the remaining questions. Set time limit of 50 minutes.	
	Upon completion of questions or time limit, again both parties note the extent to which specifications are met. They discuss their conclusions. The interviewee comments on the interview process.	
	Once again the roles are reversed and the above process completed.	
6.	Summary, back home planning	1 hr.
		8 hrs.

This learning module familiarizes the participants with the questions. It develops their confidence in using the questions. It gives them an initial experience in interpreting interview data. Thereafter, actual interviews provide the real opportunity to sharpen one's skill.

Appendix B
Skill Training in the
Performance Interview

IN OUR EXPERIENCE, instruction which makes use of role playing contributes greatly to the development of the skill of performance interviewing. A two-day learning module has proven itself. Group size should be from 12 to 21 for real skill development. The agenda for the two-day program follows:

Unit	Subject	Time
First Day		
1.	Review of group results on Coaching Practices Survey*	2½ hrs.
a.	Explanation of survey report	30 min.
b.	Small group analysis of positive and negative conditions as reflected by survey data	90 min.
c.	Small group report	30 min.

* The Coaching Practices Survey is described in a book by the author entitled *Diagnostic Studies*, published by Addison-Wesley, Reading, Mass. Data is provided on nine factors. There are seven questions for each factor.

191

Unit	Subject	Time
2.	Analysis of negative conditions ..... One negative condition is assigned to each subgroup. Each subgroup identifies the causes for the negative condition and develops a remedial action plan.	2 hrs.
3.	Report of analysis of negative conditions	1 hr.
4.	Individual analysis of own data (Process to be used is similar to that just followed for group results.)	1½ hr.
	Total	7 hrs.

Second Day

5.	Survey data implications for performance interviewing	15 min.
6.	Discussion of interview guidelines (See Chapter 7.)	45 min.
7.	Discussion of interview alternatives (See Chapter 8.)	60 min.
8.	Role playing 1 .... Groups of three, called triads, are set up with superior, subordinate, and observer assignments. Case instructions are provided for the superior and subordinates. Examples of cases which have proven themselves are included in this Appendix.	1½ hrs.
	Role playing time	30 min.
	Observer critique	15 min.
	Group discussion. Report by observer, reaction of subordinates, comments by superiors.	45 min.

Unit	Subject	Time
9.	Role playing 2 . . . . Rotate assignments. Assign new case. Follow procedure as in Unit 8.	1½ hrs.
10.	Role playing 3 . . . . Rotate assignments. Assign new case. Follow procedure as in Unit 8.	1½ hrs.
11.	Summary. Back-home action planning.	½ hr.
	Total	7 hrs.

Role Playing Cases
for
Performance Interviews

Case A   Performance interview in the absence of previously set goals.

Case B   Performance interview of the progress review type against previously set goals.

Case C   Performance interview of the annual type against previously set goals.

Case D   Performance interview of the annual type against a goals document (responsibility, indicator, goals type).

Observer's Checklist   To be used by each observer for each role play.

Performance Interview—Case A

Instructions to Superior

You have a manager working for you. He has been on the job for a year. During this time, you have had several "progress reviews." The work of his group is carried out in a satisfactory manner. He is willing to work long hours when necessary. He is very anxious to do what is right. He is conscientious. He is a pleasant chap. He seems to have potential to go further.

However, he performs poorly in one respect. He avoids making difficult decisions. He sends them in to you to make. He refers them to others. If he does make the decision, it is a very cautious, conservative decision. Often, too conservative.

You have decided to discuss this behavior with him in a thorough manner.

You want to get him to realize that he is not making the decisions he should. You plan to explore causes for this. You plan to set up some specific actions to be taken to help overcome this problem.

You asked him last week to come in for his "progress review."

Interview Preparation Steps

When your subordinate arrives, jointly select a position for him. Preferably you should take your own position. Let him take a position which might well report to you.

Identify several types of decisions the subordinate would likely be expected to make.

Do not tell him of your instructions.

Start the interview by praising results overall. No further discussion of responsibilities is called for. Then get into your discussion of his decision making.

Performance Interview—Case A

Instructions to Subordinate

You have worked for your present superior for about a year. He is helpful. He is friendly. He is willing to give you time when you need it.

You are proud of your work group. Results have been quite satisfactory.

Initially, it was somewhat difficult to make decisions, particularly about people. However, you do feel confident of your knowledge of policy and procedures. So decisions pertaining to procedures come easier for you. Your supervisor is always willing to help on the more difficult decisions. Your supervisor is known to be quick to criticize errors made by his men. You have concluded that he really prefers to make all risky decisions. If you get a chance you plan to mention this to him.

Last week, your supervisor mentioned he wanted to have a regular progress review. You look forward to finding out how you stand. You will certainly accept any suggestions he makes on improvements which are needed, although you feel all your responsibilities have been performed satisfactorily.

Interview Preparation Steps

Your supervisor will designate the position you are to assume.

Act as a manager might in a discussion with his superior, following the suggestions given above.

Performance Interview—Case B

Instructions to Superior

Assumptions:

1. You are a general manager.
2. Your subordinate is manufacturing director.
3. Your subordinate has been working for you for two years.
4. You selected him in hopes he would not only do the current job, but that he would be a potential backup for you.
5. Your subordinate prepared a set of goals (really a list of ten goals) at the beginning of the year. The goals document is attached.
6. The interview is the first quarterly review to be scheduled.
7. You have made some notes to yourself on the status of the goals (right column of goals document).
8. You are most concerned about quality (No. 2) and unit costs (No. 3).
9. In your opinion the major causes for the variances are that the subordinate:
   a. Doesn't define goals clearly enough in the beginning.
   b. Doesn't set the goals high enough.
   c. Doesn't follow up on the goals. He concentrates where he enjoys it most.
10. You hope to get acceptance of the variances as being in need of improvement. You also hope to get subordinate to accept the causes and plan appropriate remedial action.
11. You plan to follow the suggestions for progress reviews given in Chapter 8.

Performance Interview—Case B (*continued*)

Goals Document	*Notes*
1. Meet scheduled output each month, within ±10 percent.	Achieved.
2. Meet or exceed quality standards, no exception.	Missed regularly by small amount.
3. Produce results within targeted unit costs for both old and new product line.	Accomplished on old line. Missed regularly by 10 percent on new line.
4. Reduce overall costs by 10 percent.	Got up to an 8 percent rate. Seems stalled there.
5. No lost-time accidents. Downward trend on "first-aid" type accidents.	Two short interruptions. Are we lucky?
6. No downtime due to maintenance problems.	Very good record.
7. Make major changeover on production line A by end of first quarter.	Running two weeks behind schedule.
8. Conduct "state of nation" meetings with all employees in first quarter.	Accomplished. Went well. Better than last year.
9. Individual development plan prepared for each plant manager (they report to manufacturing director).	Completed. Pretty good quality.
10. Replace one plant manager by end of first quarter.	Talked about it. Hasn't bitten the bullet.

Performance Interview—Case B *(continued)*

Instructions to Subordinate

Assumptions:

1. Your superior is general manager of the division.

2. You are the manufacturing director.

3. You have been working for him for two years.

4. He selected you for your position. You anticipated working for him would be rewarding.

5. You prepared a set of goals (really a list of ten goals) at the beginning of the year. The goals document is attached.

6. You have made some notes for yourself on the status of the goals. See right column of goals document.

7. As you look at it, you have either met the goals or come close.

8. On those goals where you have come close, the causes are really attributable to other departments, particularly marketing and engineering.

9. You also feel that you and the boss didn't anticipate well in setting the original goals. In addition, your boss seems to change his priorities every month or so. One month it is quality, the next month it is costs, and so on.

10. You are looking forward to the quarterly review. You hope to have a frank discussion with the boss. You are willing to be receptive if the boss is helpful.

Performance Interview—Case B (*concluded*)

Goals Document	Notes
1. Meet scheduled output each month, within ±10 percent.	Achieved
2. Meet or exceed quality standards, no exception.	Generally achieved, have missed by small amount each month.
3. Produce results within targeted unit costs on both old and new product line.	Accomplished on old line. Missed regularly by 10 percent on new line.
4. Reduce overall costs by 10 percent.	Making steady progress. Up to 8 percent. Will get to 10 percent rate in next six months.
5. No lost-time accidents. Downward trend on "first aid" type accidents.	Very good record.
6. No downtime due to maintenance problems.	No interruptions of consequence.
7. Make major changeover on production line A by end of first quarter.	Running two weeks behind schedule.
8. Conduct "state of nation" meetings with all employees in first quarter.	Accomplished.
9. Individual development plan prepared for each plant manager (they report to manufacturing director).	Completed.
10. Replace one plant manager by end of first quarter.	Haven't done this as yet.

Performance Interview—Case C

Instructions to Superior

Assumptions:

1. You are a group officer. You have several general managers working for you. One is in charge of a division the corporation acquired two years ago. The general manager was formerly the president of the company.

2. A year ago you asked him to establish a set of goals. He did so. In spite of your efforts you couldn't get as precise goals as you would have liked.

3. You looked at the goals recently and made some notes for your annual accomplishment review.

4. You asked the subordinate to review his results for the year against his goals and come in for the annual accomplishment review.

5. You hope to get the subordinate to accept the need to improve on two critical variances.

6. When it comes to determining causes you aren't really sure what the causes are.
   a. Is the general manager upset about being acquired?
   b. Does he resent having a boss?
   c. Does he resist change?
   d. Does he resent your youthfulness?
   You just can't be sure. You hope to get a better fix on the causes.

7. In any case, you want to see some improved results.

Performance Interview—Case C (*continued*)

General Manager Goals for the Year	*Notes*
1. Sell the "old" business by the end of the third quarter. Get a "fair" price for it.	No sale. No real effort. G.M. seems relieved recently when a deal fell through.
2. Maintain the satisfactory monthly earnings record of the "old" business.	Has done this well. Seems to devote more of his time here than is deserved.
3. Avoid investing any money in the "old" business.	Didn't use any.
4. Get new plant in operation for new business by end of quarter first.	Good job. Real good team work here.
5. Have plant up to "standard" on production and quality by end of third quarter.	Missing regularly here on both. No close follow-up.
6. Upgrade the management team (two new superintendents, a new marketing man, a new personnel director).	Has done well here. Picked three (3) good men. One yet to go.
7. Complete adoption and make effective use of company's planning, budgeting, and reporting system.	Minimal progress. Low priority it seems. Probably deserved low priority in the past. Must be corrected next year.
8. Make effective use of corporate resources (capital, cash, staff know how, collaborative efforts, etc.).	No real effort made here on using staff. Seems to prefer to operate "alone."

Performance Interview—Case C (*continued*)

Instructions to Subordinate

Assumptions:

1. You have a superior who is a group officer. He has several general managers working for him. You are a general manager in charge of a company the corporation acquired two years ago. You were formerly the president of the company. The superior is a competent manager, but quite young.

2. A year ago he asked you to establish a set of goals. You did so. Being this formal made you a little uncomfortable.

3. Your superior asked you to prepare a year-end progress report against the goals. You prepared notes on your goals document to discuss with the boss. The goals for selling the "old" business were not achieved. You made some efforts, but they didn't turn out. In any case, it appears that the "old" business is a pretty good money maker, so it doesn't seem critical to sell, possibly at less than a fair price.

4. The new boss is friendly, but he seems to be a stickler for formal planning and adhering to commitments. You aren't quite sure what to expect. You hope not to get pinned down too tightly.

Performance Interview—Case C (*concluded*)

General Manager Goals for the Year	*Notes*
1. Sell the "old" business by the end of the third quarter. Get a "fair" price for it.	No sale. Three prospects. No firm offer. Still exploring.
2. Maintain the satisfactory monthly earnings record of the "old" business.	Not only maintained it. We set new records. Great year. Last quarter was off.
3. Avoid investing any money in the "old" business.	Didn't use any.
4. Get new plant in operation for new business by end of first quarter.	Opened on schedule.
5. Have plant up to "standard" on production and quality by end of third quarter.	Not close on this. Missing on both production and quality.
6. Upgrade the management team (two new superintendents, a new marketing man, a new personnel director).	Have really worked on this. Have three men. Still working on marketing.
7. Complete adoption and make effective use of company's planning, budgeting, and reporting system.	Haven't done this in "old" business. Just getting started with effort for new business.
8. Make effective use of corporate resources (capital, cash, staff know how, collaborating efforts, etc.).	Likeable chaps, but really don't know our business. We are so small and out of the way they don't seem to take much interest in us.

Performance Interview—Case D

Instructions to Superior

Your subordinate is the area supervisor for five sales persons. He has a large and dynamic area under his supervision.

Organization Chart

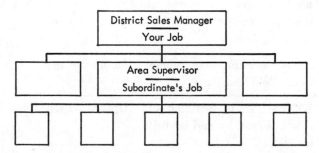

He has a degree in chemical engineering and has been with the company eight years. He took over this area about a year ago. He had previously been a salesperson in another district.

He has a group of older salespersons working for him. Some lack formal education, but all are experienced in the industry and with major customers.

You are the district sales manager to whom he reports. You selected him to be area supervisor, because he had a good knowledge of the products to be sold.

Company policy requires that all managers interview each of their subordinates once a year. The purpose of the interview is:

Evaluate performance of a subordinate and let him know how he stands.
Give recognition for work well done.
Set goals for next year.

The director of field sales, your boss, has stressed each manager's responsibility for development of his people.

Performance Interview—Case D (*continued*)

Today you have arranged to interview your subordinate.

Here is your evaluation of your subordinate:

Evaluation: Very bright, extremely good at relating to customer needs, very competent in product knowledge. Extremely hard worker, works long hours.

During the last six months there have been two occasions when results got out of control.

These occurred after a salesperson, who was regarded as a good performer, quit and it took some time to replace him, and another salesperson did not keep the area supervisor informed of price cutting activities in the field.

On both occasions he called you after the fact and told you about the difficulties.

In neither case had he investigated. In neither case did he recommend action.

Your investigation leads you to believe that in both instances, it was lack of personal review with the salesperson, along with lack of salesperson job understanding that caused the difficulty.

You plan to lay the "cards on the table" with him. *Previously, when criticized, he has always blamed others.*

In addition, you have just received an excellent expense analysis from him. However, the expense reduction effort is behind schedule. You plan to speak to him about this.

In spite of these less than desired results, you evaluate him as having potential to do an excellent job. You hope to help him in areas requiring attention and also give him encouragement to do better. He has sent you his evaluation of his performance against his goals. You are in close agreement with his own evaluation except in areas already noted above.

Performance Evaluation
of Subordinate

Goals for the Year	*Evaluation*
1. *Sales*	
a. Sell 20,000,000 pounds of chemical A, divided among five salespersons.	*a.* Actual sales, 19,200,000 pounds. Three salespersons made goals, one achieved 80 percent of goal. One salesperson terminated in June.
b. Sell 250,000 pounds of compound B.	*b.* Actual sales, 260,000 pounds. Three salespersons exceeded goals, price cutters took 50 percent of business of other salespersons.
c. Sell 10,000,000 pounds of chemical C, divided among five salespersons.	*c.* Actual sales, 9,600,000 pounds. One salesperson made goal, three made 95 percent of goals, other salesperson quit.
2. *Staffing*	
a. Train or recruit backup personnel so that no vacancy remains unfilled more than ten working days.	*a.* Salesperson's job open three months.
3. *Pricing*	
a. Permit no sales below approved schedules.	*a.* None made without prior review with district manager.

Performance Interview—Case D (*continued*)

Goals for the Year	*Evaluation*
4. Expenses	
a. None exceed budget for year.	*a.* Two percent over budget with heavier expenses early in year than anticipated.
b. Complete analysis and reduction plan for control of expense by given date.	*b.* Comprehensive reduction plan submitted prior to this date.
5. Sales planning	
a. Forecast sales within 2 percent of actual.	*a.* Total sales within 4 percent of forecast for following reasons: three salespersons achieved goals, one within 15 percent of actual, other quit unexpectedly and it took time to replace him.
6. Market intelligence	
a. No major competitive surprises in territory.	*a.* No surprises, unusually good job, found out about Standard Chemicals new product, Zerone, before other districts.
7. Safety	
a. No lost-time accidents in office.	*a.* None.
b. No more than two minor injuries.	*b.* Had only one.
c. No auto damage claims or injuries on road.	*c.* One salesperson had minor accident on Freeway, but lost no time. $250 claim.

Performance Interview—Case D (*continued*)

8. *Personnel development*

    a. Follow plan for all salespersons.   *a.* Done.

    b. Follow personal plan.   *b.* Done.

9. *Relationships*

    a. No more than three occasions when district manager becomes involved in differences between area supervisor or product managers.   *a.* Only one instance reported.

    b. *Follow personal* provided to plant on customer complaints.   *b.* Only two second requests for additional information in the year. Neither appeared justified.

Performance Interview—Case D (*continued*)

Instructions for Subordinate

You are an area supervisor. You have five salespersons working for you. You have a large and dynamic area under your supervision.

Organization Chart

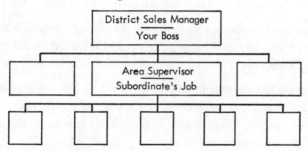

You have a degree in chemical engineering and have been with the company eight years. You took over this area about a year ago. You have previously been a salesperson in another district.

You have a group of older salespersons working for you. Some lack formal education, but all are experienced in the industry and with major customers.

Your boss is the district sales manager. He selected you to be area supervisor because you had a good knowledge of the products to be sold.

Company policy requires that all managers interview each of their subordinates once a year. The purpose of the interview is:

Evaluate performance of subordinates and let them know how they stand.

Give recognition for work well done.

Set goals for next year.

Performance Interview—Case D (*continued*)

The director of field sales, to whom your boss reports, has stressed each manager's responsibility for development of his people.

When your boss gave you the job he said it was going to be a *challenge*. It has been. Improvement has been difficult. Some "bugs" developed. The problems have taxed the ability of your salespersons. You have had to work long hard hours. However, you did get things *running satisfactorily by the end of the year*.

On two occasions last year things got out of control, when a salesperson quit and when price cutting occurred in the territory. Your boss criticized you at the time for not acting sooner.

You pointed out that these possibilities had been well planned for by you. However, lack of communication with your salespersons caused the problem. You consider this to be the fault of the salesperson, not you.

In addition, your boss has been stressing expense reduction efforts. You have completed a very complete analysis of expenses. This analysis has just been sent to him.

Last week your boss mentioned it was time for the annual performance interview. It shouldn't take too long, but it's nice to have the boss tell you about the job you are doing. Maybe there is a raise in it; maybe he will tell you about what to expect in the future.

Your boss asked you to review your accomplishment of goals and evaluate how successful your results were. You have just done this. He asked you to send him a copy of the performance evaluation, which you have done.

Performance Interview—Case D (*continued*)

Performance Evaluation
of Subordinate

Goals for the Year	*Evaluation*
1. *Sales*	
a. Sell 20,000,000 pounds of chemical A, divided among five salespersons.	*a.* Actual sales, 19,200,000 pounds. Three salespersons made goals; one achieved 80 percent of goal. One salesperson terminated in June.
b. Sell 250,000 pounds of compound B.	*b.* Actual sales, 260,000 pounds. Three salespersons exceeded goals, price cutters took 50 percent of business of others.
c. Sell 10,000,000 pounds of chemical C, divided among five salespersons.	*c.* Actual sales, 9,600,000 pounds. One made goal, three made 95 percent of goals, other salesperson quit.
2. *Staffing*	
a. Train or recruit backup personnel so that no vacancy remains unfilled more than ten working days.	*a.* Salesperson's job open three months.
3. *Pricing*	
a. Permit no sales below approved schedules.	*a.* None made without prior review with district manager.

Performance Interview—Case D (*continued*)

Goals for the Year	*Evaluation*
4. *Expenses*	
a. None exceed budget for year.	*a.* Two percent over budget with heavier expenses early in year than anticipated.
b. Complete analysis and improvement plan for control of expense by given date.	*b.* Comprehensive improvement plan submitted prior to date.
5. *Sales planning*	
a. Forecast sales within 2 percent of actual.	*a.* Total sales within 4 percent of forecast for following reasons: three salespersons achieved goals, one within 15 percent of actual, other quit unexpectedly and it took time to replace him.
6. *Market intelligence*	
a. No major competitive surprises in territory.	*a.* No surprises, unusually good job, found out about Standard Chemicals new product Zerone, before other districts.
7. *Safety*	
a. No lost-time accidents in office.	*a.* None.
b. No more than two injuries.	*b.* Had only one.
c. No auto damage claims or injuries on road.	*c.* One salesperson had minor accident on Freeway, but lost no time. $250 claim.

8. *Personnel development*

    a. Follow plan for all salespersons.   *a.* Done.

    b. Follow personal plan.   *b.* Done.

9. *Relationships*

    a. No more than three occasions when district manager becomes involved in differences between area supervisor or product managers.   *a.* Only one instance reported.

    b. Full information provided to plant on customer complaints.   *a.* Only two second requests for additional information in the year. Neither appeared justified.

Observer's Check List

Instructions: Make notes as interview proceeds so you can answer questions below. Select the *one* coaching interview suggestion done *best* and the one needing most attention in future interviews.

1. *Coach on results:*
    Were results stressed or were traits stressed?
    If traits were stressed, were they related to end results?
    Was criticism personal or job centered?

2. *Get down to cases:*
    How specific were the reasons given by the superior for his opinions?
    Were specific incidents used well?
    How frank was the superior?

3. *Determine causes:*
    Was an attempt made to get at causes?
    Did they get at several causes?
    Did they get at the real cause(s)?

4. *Make interview a two-way process:*
    Was the supervisor dominant?
    Who did the most talking?
    Was there good give-and-take discussion?
    Were questions used to stimulate thinking?

5. Set or reset goals or targets:
    Were goals set against which subordinate could measure his own progress?
    Were goals specific or general?
    Were goals imposed or developed jointly?

6. *Provide motivation:*
    Did superior evidence concern about subordinate?
    Did superior use positive or negative motivation?
    Was the subordinate motivated to act differently in the future?

Appendix C
Skill Training in the
Counseling Interview

DEVELOPING SKILL in the counseling interview, in our experience, can be done by effective use of role playing. We have developed a one-day learning module, the agenda for which follows:

Unit	Subject	Time
1.	Discussion of counseling principles (Chapter 9) ....1 hr.	
2.	Discussion of the counseling interview process (Chapter 10) ....1 hr.	
3.	Role playing 1 ....1½ hrs. Triads are used. Cases are assigned in terms of participants' previously stated problems. Case studies follow following timing:	

<table>
<tr><td></td><td>Preparation ....10 min.</td></tr>
<tr><td></td><td>Role playing ....30 min.</td></tr>
<tr><td></td><td>Observer critique ....20 min.</td></tr>
<tr><td></td><td>Group discussion ....30 min.</td></tr>
</table>

4.	Role playing 2 ....1½ hrs. Rotate triad. Assign appropriate case. Same timing as in Role #1.	
5.	Role playing 3 ....1½ hrs. Rotate triad. Assign appropriate case. Same timing.	
6.	Summary. Back-home action planning. ......½ hr.
	Total ....7 hrs.	

Role Playing Cases
for
Counseling Interviews

Case 1 Subordinate is a young staff manager. He is ambitious. He is capable. His relations with his fellow members of supervision is quite ineffective. This destroys team play and will hold him back if he continues.

Case 2 Subordinate is an experienced employee who appears to have a drinking problem.

Case 3 Subordinate is capable in getting results but is verbose in expression; his sense of humor also gets misunderstood.

Case 4 Old-timer who feels entitled to special considerations.

Observer's Checklist

Counseling Case 1

Instructions to Subordinate

You have a relatively young man working for you in a staff position. He has worked for you for two years. He is a very capable, hard-working young man. He masters new assignments so readily he has been given a series of trouble-shooting assignments. These he has done well. He is extremely bright.

In spite of these very excellent characteristics, he has one habit which is not desirable.

His relations with fellow members of management are not effective. Friction exists. The other members of management avoid him, they are seldom cooperative. Several have mentioned to you that the young man implied that they are stupid.

The young man on several occasions has taken delight in showing up errors or weaknesses of his colleagues to you.

You have decided that the young man's habits are detrimental to the team work you must have in your group.

You scheduled today for a discussion with him. Unfortunately, you have only a limited time for the interview. You realize you can't accomplish everything you want to in this short period of time.

Preparation Steps

Assume you are in your current position. Have your subordinate assume a position reporting to you.

Don't discuss your instructions with the subordinate. The time for the interview will be announced.

Instructions to Subordinate

You have worked for your current superior for two years. You were delayed in your career by military duty. You hope that you can progress rapidly. You became a manager about a year ago (use another title if it would be more appropriate to do so). You have secured a college degree by going to school nights.

Your supervisor is a pleasant individual to work for. He expects results. He stresses team work. However, you notice you seem to get the tough assignments. In fact, you have had several in the last year. You completed them satisfactorily.

Your superior asked you to come in for a discussion about your work. You are not sure what he intends to cover. You feel you are ready for a promotion. You are concerned that someone may be holding you back. You are looking forward to the discussion.

If your superior gives you criticism, you will ask for supporting illustrations. You pride yourself on "looking facts in the face." If your superior provides specific examples for any criticism you will listen. If he doesn't you will ask for evidence, politely, of course. The more interest your superior shows in your ambitions, the more attentive you will be to his suggestions. You hope to get some indication of whether or not you have promotional opportunities ahead.

Preparation Steps

Your superior will assume his current position. The two of you should select a position reporting to him for you to fill.

Counseling Case 2

Background

You have a group of very experienced employees working for you. They are quite competent. They work quite independently. They require little supervision.

Recently you have become concerned about one man. He began to take long lunch hours. On several occasions it became apparent to you and others he had been drinking at lunch. While not serious yet, you notice he has been absent on Monday on several occasions. As far as the record reveals, he has seldom been absent before. The quality of his work has held up. His productivity when on the job is very good.

You had a brief chat with him last week to express concern about him and about his record. He promised to do better in the future.

Yesterday was another long lunch hour. Today when he returned from a long lunch hour, he obviously had been drinking. You asked him to come into your office for a talk.

Counseling Case 2 (*continued*)

Instructions to Subordinate

You have been in your current position quite some time. You are an "expert" at your particular work. You are proud of both the quality and quantity of your work.

At one time you had hoped to get promoted. A promotion seems to be less likely now.

At one time you had a superior who was quite friendly. The current one seems to be quite distant.

Some time ago you found it necessary to take a cocktail at lunch. Recently, it seems that two are better than one. However, you don't let anything interfere with either the quality or quantity of your work.

Today you had several cocktails. You happened to meet your superior at the elevator when you came back about 2:30 P.M. He asked you to come to his office. You are not quite sure what to expect.

Counseling Case 3

Instructions to Superior

You have a very competent individual working for you. (Decide before starting what position he holds as a manager.) He has worked for you for about a year. The work of his group is up to standard in all respects.

However, he does have one characteristic which is most aggravating to you and to others with whom he works. In both written and oral expression, he is verbose. He takes twice the time it should to say something.

This habit is not only irritating, it means time is wasted. It also means that the subordinate's "image" upstairs is not as positive as it might well be, in light of the good performance results.

In addition, in some meetings with higher level managers the subordinate has on several occasions made humorous comments which were not appreciated. They led to higher level managers assuming he isn't serious about his responsibilities. As one said, "He's too much of a clown."

Preparation Steps

Assume your own position.

Assign a position title to your new "subordinate."

Do not share instructions.

The time for the interview will be announced.

Counseling Case 3 (*continued*)

Instructions to Subordinate

You have worked for your current superior for about a year. You are proud of the results you have gotten. They are up to standard, if not better.

You are anxious to make a good showing since promotional opportunities may be coming up in the near future.

Your superior has indicated he wants to talk with you about your performance. If he gives you any suggestions for improvement, you certainly will try to profit from them.

You have always endeavored to provide comprehensive answers to questions. You plan to do the same for any questions your superior raises.

Counseling Case 4

Instructions to Superior

You have a group of high-level specialists who work for you. Some are "old-timers," some are young men.

You were appointed manager over this group about two years ago.

You have had a long-standing problem with some of the old-timers. They feel that they are entitled to special considerations (such as personal calls, leaving early, long lunches, etc.).

One individual leaves early on occasion without either telling you or requesting permission. In addition, he seems to be making frequent personal telephone calls (it seems like calls to his broker).

Another man, in particular, has been a frequent violator. You have decided you must talk to the men who are violators. You have asked the more frequent violator to come in for a talk. You plan to explain to him that some of his habits will have to change.

Instructions to Subordinate

You are a high-level specialist. You have been with the organization for many years. You feel that you are entitled to special considerations. You do your work well. Your productivity is high. So occasionally you leave early. Once in a while you do make a call to your stockbroker.

Your previous superior permitted you to do this. However, your new supervisor seems to be tightening up on privileges, and so forth. You feel your long experience should entitle you to some consideration.

Your new superior has just asked you to come in to talk with him.

Observer's Checklist for Counseling Interviews

Questions	*Notes*
1. Was purpose of interview stressed initially? Was stress placed on helping subordinate?	
2. Was the undesirable attitude or behavior stated in specific terms?	
3. Was subordinate given full opportunity to talk?	
4. Did subordinate accept need to change?	
5. Were any specific actions planned?	
6. Was follow-up provided?	
7. Which counseling principles were well applied?	

Appendix D
Skill Training in the
Career Discussion

DEVELOPING skill in career discussions does require skill training. We rely upon role playing. A one-day learning experience follows the agenda below:

Unit	Subject	Time
1.	Presentation on career discussion principles (Chapter 11).	1 hr.
2.	Presentation of career discussion alternatives (Chapter 12).	1 hr.
3.	Role playing 1 .... Similar process and timing is used as for counseling interviews.	1½ hrs.
4.	Role playing 2 (Similar process as for No. 1)	1½ hrs.
5.	Role playing 3 (Similar process as for No. 2)	1½ hrs.
6.	Summary and back-home planning.	½ hr.
	Total	7 hrs.

Role Playing Cases
for
Career Discussions

Case 1 Exploratory discussion. Subordinate verbalizes high ambitions, but is reluctant to make sacrifices.

Case 2 Career discussion (general). Superior hopes to get subordinate to accept shift from line to staff position.

Case 3 Career discussion (general). Subordinate has plateaued. Superior desires to get this accepted.

Case 4 Career discussion (specific). Superior wants subordinate to be his backup. Subordinate satisfied where he is.

Case 5 Career discussion (specific). Superior has to ask subordinate to take a sideways move.

Case 6 Career discussion (general). Superior not likely to get promoted to general manager position.

Observer Checklist

Case 1—Superior

Instructions

You have had a Coaching Practices Survey that says your subordinates all want a career discussion. You asked your subordinates to complete a Developmental Dialogue No. 2 Worksheet. You have saved the most difficult one for last.

The subordinate expresses a strong interest in getting promoted. Yet he is reluctant to move geographically.

He hasn't evidenced an interest in mastering other functions.

He is reluctant to take a lateral move.

He also insists on undue precision. He wants to know just when he will be promoted, and so forth.

You hope to get the subordinate to be much more realistic about the future.

If he doesn't change his attitude regarding the restraints, he has little or no opportunity for promotion.

Since he is a capable performer and has much knowledge of value to competition, you don't want to lose him.

Career Case 1—Subordinate

Instructions

Your superior has told everyone he will hold a career discussion. This pleases you because you have many questions you want to ask him. You are particularly anxious because your wife keeps bugging you on your next move. She says the company doesn't appreciate you.

You have completed a Development Dialogue Worksheet at the request of your superior. You hope to really pin him down on whether it is performance or politics which counts.

You hope to get specifics on when you will be promoted.

DEVELOPMENTAL DIALOGUE FORM #2

This form has been designed to give you an opportunity to discuss those aspects of your future which are of most interest and importance to you. Please feel free to express how you view your immediate and long-range plans.

In this way you can be assisted in setting realistic goals for the future. The value of this information depends on the frankness and care with which you answer the questions.

Name _*Yourself*_

Date Completed _*Yesterday*_

1. How do you feel about your career progress to date?

   Not too good. I feel I have been stymied.
   Others my age are a level or two higher.

2. What is the next position you hope to fill in the Company?

   I would like to fill my boss's shoes next.
   It's the job I'm best qualified for.

3. Realistically, you are in competition for promotional
   opportunities. You have some competitive advantages,
   you have some competitive disadvantages. What do
   you believe them to be?

Advantages	Disadvantages
- Ambitious	- Have been in one job
- Highly intelligent	and one location
- Know my function	too long.
- Well liked	
- Get results	- Not a politician

4. What can be done to overcome or minimize the disadvantages?

   Can't move because my wife works.
   Hate to think I have to become a politician.

5. It sometimes helps to think longer range about one's career.
   For example, what kind of work do you hope to be doing
   five years from now?

   Hope to be at least two levels
   above where I am now.

6. How can you best prepare so that you can achieve your ambitions?

   I have understudied my boss closely.
   Maybe I should go to some management
   course. My boss has recently done so.

7. Are there any considerations, such as location, change in
   location, amount of traveling, family needs which must be
   taken into account over the next five years?

   Yes. I don't see the need to move. In
   fact, I can't move because of my wife.
   I am willing to travel. I think I am
   ready. According to my "PERT Chart"
   I'm three years behind my career
   schedule. Frankly, I need to have
   assurances of a future with this Company.

Career Case 2—Supervisor

The subordinate is a manager in his late thirties. He has been with the company for 16 years. He has received several promotions. In his most recent position he now supervises a large work force. You were brought into the division to make a major increase in efficiency. After thorough study, you assessed this manager. In your last appraisal interview with him you appraised him as doing "less than adequate" on the direct supervision of his work force. He doesn't seem to be a natural leader. He is good at planning, he comes up with brilliant new methods and procedures, but when it comes to motivating his group to really produce for him he doesn't do it. As a result of the interview, the subordinate said he would try to improve but six months have gone by and no improvement is forthcoming.

You have decided that the subordinate's future lies in a staff assignment. You have need for such an individual. The new position would pay as well as the current one. You have called the subordinate in for an initial discussion.

Preparation Steps

1. Assume your own position. Assign subordinate to a position which would report directly to you.

2. Do not reveal your instructions.

3. You hope to get the subordinate to accept the shift to a staff assignment. You plan to make use of a check-list of position requirements.

4. You will have 20–30 minutes to complete this initial career discussion.

A Checklist of Position Requirements or Position Specifications

1. *Experience required*
   a. Total amount of pertinent experience.
   b. Amount of supervisory experience.

2. *Technical knowledge*
   a. Areas requiring complete familiarity.
   b. Areas requiring general familiarity.

3. *Education or advanced training required*

4. *Managerial ability*
   Planning
   Organizing
   Motivating
   Ability to delegate
   Ability to develop subordinates
   Controlling

5. *Mental abilities*

6. *Personal motivation*

7. *Personality characteristics*
   Aggressiveness
   Judgment
   Emotional Stability
   Expression (oral and writing ability)
   Analytical
   Self-confidence
   Ability to work through others
   Character and integrity

8. *Physical*
   Health

9. *Special requirements*

Career Case 2—Subordinate

You are 38 years of age and have been working for the company for 16 years. You have received several promotions and now supervise a fairly large group. After several years on this job you are quite sure that you want to climb up the management ladder. Planning is the essence of good management and this is your long suit. The direct supervision of the work force is not so exciting, but this is something you can always get an assistant to do for you.

Recently, the division got a new manager who seems to be quite demanding.

In your last discussion with him on your performance the boss rated you down on ability to supervise. You didn't argue too much with him at the time although you didn't fully agree with him. You promised that he would see an improvement and there has been some, but it comes pretty slow.

Your superior asked you to come in for a six-month followup discussion. Likely he will stress the need for further improvement in your supervision of the work force. You plan to get as many suggestions as you can from him and then do your best to put them into effect.

Preparation Steps

1. Your superior will give you the title of your now position. It will be one which reports to him directly.

2. Do not reveal your instructions to your superior.

3. You are just arriving in the boss's office. He has scheduled 30 minutes for the interview.

Career Case 3—Superior

This subordinate has worked for you for six years. He is 56 years of age. During your appraisal interview held two weeks ago, he indicated he would like to talk about the requirements for getting promoted.

You are satisfied with his performance on his current job and would like to see him complete his career where he is. Unfortunately, you are just about out of carrots. He is almost to the top of his salary range.

Basically, you would like to get him to see that he is not likely to get promoted, but to keep him motivated to go on doing a good job in his current position. The next logical jobs to which he aspires require a great deal more technical sophistication than he possesses or is likely to acquire.

You provided him with the position requirements for these jobs and asked him to study them before the interview. You plan to use them in helping him be realistic.

Career Case 3—Subordinate

You have worked for your superior for six years. Although you realize a technical background is required for the next logical step up from your present job, you feel your vast PRACTICAL experience qualifies you. You emphasize PRACTICAL.

You mentioned your ambition to your superior during your appraisal interview and he agreed to talk to you about your future. This is important to you. You are 56 years of age. You have one son in college and another ready to enter next year. The mortgage on your home must be kept up, and the payments on the new car need to be paid.

You plan to bring up these points to illustrate your need for the promotion.

Your superior gave you a copy of position requirements for the next higher jobs. You feel you are basically qualified except for the educational requirements (technical).

A Checklist of Position Requirements or Position Specifications

1. *Experience required*
   a. Total amount of pertinent experience.
   b. Amount of supervisory experience.

2. *Technical knowledge*
   a. Areas requiring complete familiarity.
   b. Areas requiring general familiarity.

3. *Education or advanced training required*

4. *Managerial ability*
   Planning
   Organizing
   Motivating
   Ability to delegate
   Ability to develop subordinates
   Controlling

5. *Mental abilities*

6. *Personal motivation*

7. *Personality characteristics*
   Aggressiveness
   Judgment
   Emotional stability
   Expression (oral and writing ability)
   Analytical
   Self-confidence
   Ability to work through others
   Character and integrity

8. *Physical*
   Health

9. *Special requirements*

Career Case 4—Superior

This subordinate has worked for you for five years. Although he does adequately on most of his responsibilities and even exceptionally well on some, he does not seem to be developing rapidly enough toward the point at which he would be ready for your job. He is particularly poor in planning jobs, which often results in lost time or extra work. You recall several such instances.

The chances for your promotion have caused you to become more and more concerned about your replacement. This subordinate would be your choice over others working for you.

You have established as one of your objectives that of motivating the subordinate to put forth more effort to get ready for your job.

You can't promise him anything, but you want him to know his future is tied directly to his performance.

Two days ago you asked him if he would come in at this time for an interview.

Career Case 4—Subordinate

You have worked for your superior for five years. You enjoy your job. It consumes just eight daily hours of your time and leaves plenty of opportunity to enjoy your several hobbies.

You often feel sorry for your boss who seems to be working extremely long hours.

Although you are not yet 40, you and your wife have talked things over and agreed that you both would be satisfied if you stayed right where you are.

You are sure your performance is satisfactory and that your boss holds you in high regard.

Two days ago your boss asked you to come in at this time for an interview. You are not sure what this means, but you have no apprehensions.

Career Case 5—Superior

You have a subordinate who is doing a satisfactory job where he is. In fact, it is quite satisfactory. However, he isn't going to go any further. He knows it. You know it.

Recently it has become increasingly apparent that you must have a competent backup. The best place for such an individual is in this subordinate's position. You have decided to ask him to move sideways. You won't have to cut his pay, but the new assignment is not the prestige job the present one is. You have asked your subordinate to come in.

You hope to get him to accept the necessity of the change and still be motivated to perform well.

Career Case 5—Subordinate

You have been in your present position for quite some time. You haven't really had a good talk with your boss about your future, but you have about concluded that you aren't going any further.

You hope to be able to stay in your present job. You have worked hard to establish a good performance record. You are a bit apprehensive about the "young tiger" program. It seems younger men are often brought in and competent older men pushed to one side.

Your boss has said he wants to talk with you. He really didn't say what about.

Instructions to Supervisor

You are a general manager. Due to reorganization, a considerable number of changes have been made in the supervisory and managerial personnel.

One particular manager has stayed right where he was in the beginning. He hasn't been promoted. He hasn't been demoted. His overall performance is very satisfactory. He has been a manager for five years. However, he doesn't meet the qualifications which your department manager and division manager now require of new general managers. You were asked to complete a Promotability Checklist on him. A copy is attached. He missed on two significant items: managerial ability, and expression (oral and written).

You had a regular performance interview with this manager. During the discussion, the manager indicated he was quite concerned about his future. He asked for an opportunity to talk with you. You have scheduled such a career discussion for today.

You want to see what concerns the manager has. You can't hold any hope for him getting a promotion. On the other hand, you want him to be motivated to continue to do his current job and do it well.

Preparation Steps

1. Assume you're a general manager.

2. Assign your subordinate to a position as a manager. You might pick an actual position if you wish.

3. Do not reveal your instructions.

4. The subordinate has been asked to come in for a discussion with you about his career.

5. You will have about 25 minutes to complete this initial career discussion.

Promotability Checklist

		Assessment
1.	*Experience required*	
	a. Total amount of pertinent experience.	More than enough.
	b. Amount of supervisory experience	Five years at 2nd level.
2.	*Technical knowledge*	
	a. Areas requiring complete familiarity.	Very good grasp of the work itself, and the company.
	b. Areas requiring general familiarity.	
3.	*Education or advanced training required*	Hasn't got a degree.
4.	*Managerial ability*	
	Planning	
	Organizing	Satisfactory at manager
	Motivating	level, but not strong for
	Ability to delegate	a general manager posi-
	Ability to develop subordinates	tion.
	Controlling	
5.	*Mental abilities*	Quite satisfactory.
6.	*Personal motivation*	Quite satisfactory.
7.	*Personal characteristics*	
	Aggressiveness	Satisfactory
	Judgment	Satisfactory
	Emotional Stability	Satisfactory
	Expression (oral and written ability)	A liability of consequence
	Analytical	Satisfactory
	Self-confidence	Satisfactory

	Assessment
Ability to work through others	Satisfactory
Character and integrity	No question
8. *Physical*	
Health	Good
Appearance	Good
9. *Overall appraisal of pro-motability for promotion*	Has two serious limitations as a potential general manager. Don't think he can qualify.

Career Case 6—Subordinate

Instructions to Subordinate

You are a manager. Your department has been through a re-organization. However, you neither got promoted nor down-graded. In fact, you didn't have a discussion with anybody. This left you quite concerned. So in your last performance interview you ask your general manager for an opportunity to talk about your career.

You certainly don't want to be surprised by a demotion. You certainly believe that you can do a bigger job.

If they are going to leave you at current level, at least you would like to be shifted around now and then to avoid boredom or going stale.

You have been a manager for five years.

As you look at some of the promotions, you are convinced you are as capable as those who got the promotions. Admittedly, you didn't get to complete college because you had to go to work. However, you certainly know the work, itself, as well as anybody.

Preparation Steps

1. Assume you are a manager. Your general manager may well ask you to assume you are in an actual position.

2. Do not reveal your instructions to your manager.

3. In case of a difference of opinion on a fact, your manager is to establish the fact.

4. You are just arriving at the general manager's office. He has scheduled 25 minutes for the interview.

Observer Checklist for Career Discussion

Questions	*Notes*

1. Was concern evidenced for subordinate?
    At very beginning?
    Thereafter?	

2. Were organizational necessities stressed in straightforward manner?	

3. Did superior have a good fix on needs of subordinate?
    Aspirations for advancement?
    Job-oriented needs?
      (status, power, etc.)
    Others?	

4. *Realism* Did superior help subordinate to be more realistic? Was superior realistic about subordinate?	
5. *Individual versus specifications* Were specifications used effectively? Were comparisons with others avoided? Did both parties agree on the specifications? Did both parties agree on extent to which specifications were met?	
6. *Action planning* Where appropriate, were action plans specific on who, what and when?	

Index

Index

Specifications
  career discussion in terms of, 165–67
  preparation of, 77–80
  types of, 67–77, 97–98
  use of, 80–81, 89–90, 98–100, 153–54
Specificity, 113–14
Standards, 135–36
Status, 44
Stress, 131–32
Success, feeling of, 39–43
Successful group, 42

Superior-subordinate relationships, 2, 5–32
Supervision, 94

Terkel, Studs, 35–37

Willingness, 47–49
Work
  addiction, 37, 45
  interesting, 33–34
  meaning of, 34–37
  as self-validation, 37